The Great Canadian Road

Toronto — 1977

Red Rock Publishing Co. Limited

The Great Canadian Road

a history of Yonge Street

Jay Myers

THE GREAT CANADIAN ROAD
a history of Yonge Street

Designed and typeset by Roberts & Johnson

Jacket design by Tom Sankey

Canadian Cataloguing in Publication Data.

Myers, Jay, 1949-
    The great Canadian road

Bibliography: p.
Includes index.
ISBN 0-920178-02-2

1. Toronto, Ont. - Streets - Yonge Street -
History. 1. Title.

FC3097.67.M93 1977   971.3'541   C77-001335-X
F1059.5.T6875Y65 1977

Red Rock Publishing Co. Limited
170 Bloor Street W., Suite 419
Toronto, Canada M4S 1T9

first printing 1977

Cushing, Harvey

This road is now the celebrated Yonge Street, said to be the longest "street" in the world, though for many years after it was projected it scarcely deserved even the name of trail.

The Life of Sir William Osler (1925)
Colombo's Canadian Quotations (1974)

for Sam and Mildred Myers

. . . with a special thanks to Pauline Rhind for giving me the opportunity to write; to Duncan Pollock for just being there; and to Elaine who cared from the beginning.

CONTENTS

Major Indian Trails 1

I N THE BEGINNING, billowing funnels of gray smoke rising from
bark wigwams were the only signs of life. Beyond that, there was
the unexplored territory of wild animals — and in every direction
the permeating and ever-present wind-creaked silence interrupted only
by the calls of the many birds native to the region.

Red and white pine trees, six-feet in diameter, some five hundred
years old, others as tall as a 17-storey office building, shut out most
of the sunshine. It was a land where bears, wolves and panthers
encountered the silver fox, lynx, marten and the woodland jumping
mouse.

Long before the drone of sawmills, tollgates, stage coach
travel, tarred roads, fast cars, subways, shopping malls and nude
body-rub parlours, a dense and pathless forest reflected in the cool
waters of Toronto Harbour.

Yet while the long and unbroken line of woods may have
radiated gloom and loneliness, it also evoked great visions in the
minds of the men who were soon to take root in the new land.

The dog's-tooth violet, fleur-de-lis, white water lily, honeysuckle,
wild rose and sweet briar would see the glitter of sharp steel
swung by the hands of strange men in a strange and new land,
men who would take their place in history because they had a
dream, a dream that became a reality through dogged determination.

These were the men who fashioned the route that is now the
longest street in the world — Yonge Street. Indian scouts, explorers,
soldiers, sailors, governors, pedlars, bandits, settlers all played a part
in one of the greatest sagas of Canadian history.

Beneath the mysterious tree tops were three major Indian
trails which figured in the development of the great Yonge Street

route: the Rouge Trail, Don Trail and Humber Trail, all of which terminated at the south end of Lake Simcoe on the lower branches of the Holland River.

As early as 1650, one map outlined the Humber-Holland Trail or portage; the most direct route north through the Great Lakes region. It was a 28-mile winding portage trail leading from the Southern Ontario woods, through the twists and curves of the Humber River, over hills, gulleys and swamps, to the Holland River. A narrow footpath carved through the raw forest by the never-ending drive of feet, it was a trail that lead to the Upper Lakes of Huron and Georgian Bay, near the present site of Penetanguishene, known by several names: The Humber Trail, the Humber-Holland Portage, the Pass at Toronto, the Toronto Portage, le Passage de Toronto, le Portage de Toronto and the Toronto Carrying-Place; it was a trail well-known long before the white man first travelled it — its origins went back to the earliest years of human life in North America.

The old trail began at the mouth of the Humber River (once known as the Toronto River or St. John's River), where it flows into Lake Ontario, up the river's east bank to the present site of Nobleton, then across the east branch of the Humber River northward to the west branch of the Holland River (or Micicaguean Creek). From there it was possible to paddle by canoe to Lake Simcoe, then across it and Lake Couchiching into Georgian Bay by way of the Severn River and several portages.

A wild and illiterate character named Etienne Brûlé was the first European to make his way west of the Ottawa River, and the first white man to use the Humber-Holland route in the early part of the seventeenth century. This young Frenchman, a brilliant explorer and one of Champlain's leading young lieutenants, made many a trading and fishing trip with the Huron Indians who called this pathway "To'ron'to".

Toronto was the name given to that region between Lake Ontario and Lake Simcoe — a place of rendezvous for many Indian tribes.

In the winter of 1615-16, Champlain himself portaged along the trail to the Holland River, paddled his canoe down the river into Lake Simcoe, then portaged along what is now the Coldwater road from Orillia to Warminster, where the Huron village of Cahiaque was located.

Others who travelled the great portage included Joliet, Denonville and St. Jean de Brébeuf.

2

La Salle saw the Toronto Carrying-Place three times in 1680 and 1681, when he transported arms and equipment to and from the Mississippi into the Illinois country.

Here too could be seen the black robes of the Jesuits, the Récollets and the French pioneers. Dutchmen from the Hudson reached Lake Ontario by way of the trail, as did the French traders from Fort Frontenac, and the lawless *coureurs-de-bois* from the St. Lawrence. These characters were bush rangers of the French regime, adventurous, lusty men who lived a hard life in a rugged land.

In the early fur trading days of exploration, the French capitalists in Montreal, also known as the "pedlars from Quebec", formed companies to develop the fur trade business. They sent their hard-working agents to distant regions of the country to expand the company's operations.

In exchange for the valuable skins of the beaver, mink, fox and otter which were most abundant in the upper lakes of Huron and Georgian Bay, the Indians received such "valuables" as knives, beads and liquor. There was a great deal of money to be made in this business. The fur trade had been a great source of wealth during the French regime, giving employment to a large number of skilled traders and voyageurs. It developed under the direction of a group of shrewd Scottish merchants in Montreal, known as the North West Company, who entered into eager rivalry with the Hudson's Bay Company on the north, and the traders of New York on the south. In 1783, this North West Company began to explore new routes to the west and turned their attention to Toronto and the Toronto Carrying-Place.

There were four main routes to the upper lakes from Quebec. The most common journey was by way of the Ottawa and French Rivers to Georgian Bay; but this route meant that the rich supplies of furs all along the southern end of the St. Lawrence, Lake Ontario and Lake Erie were neglected.

Some fur traders preferred a more southerly route, on the St. Lawrence to Lake Ontario, then on to the Trent River and the chain of lakes and streams winding their way to Georgian Bay. But this was also a difficult journey with many portages.

One particular trading post established on the island of Michilimackinac (now Mackinaw or the Mackinac), situated on the northwesterly tip of the southern shore of Lake Huron at the entrance to Lake Michigan, was the furthest point of exploration of the French voyageurs and soon became the western centre of the fur trade.

Those wishing to reach the trading post at Michilimackinac could travel by way of the Niagara River. Traders would journey south on the St. Lawrence River to Lake Ontario and on to the mouth of the Niagara River leading into Lake Erie. From there they would travel to the western end of Lake Erie, where the Detroit and St. Clair Rivers would take them into Lake Huron.

There still remained a more direct route to Michilimackinac and the upper lakes. This was via the Humber River and the Humber-Holland Portage or Trail. Three-foot wide canoes were lugged over the long portage and hilly ground between Teiaiagon, an old Seneca Indian village and trading post at the mouth of the Humber River, and Lake Simcoe.

As the fur trading industry in Montreal became a major commercial success, steps were considered which would yield a shorter and safer route to the distant trading posts.

One of these was the idea of building a road from Lake Ontario all the way north to Lake Simcoe through the woods. As early as 1784, Benjamin Frobisher, one of the active partners of the North West Company, wrote a letter to Henry Hamilton, Governor of Quebec (1782-1785): "I have . . . laid it down in the enclosed sketch . . . to show that there is such a road."[1]

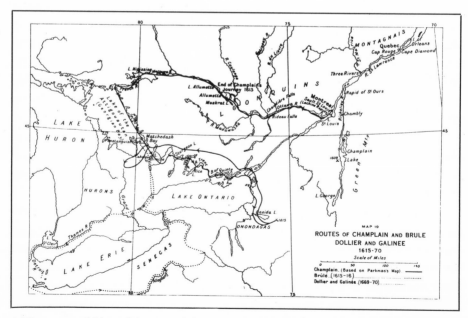

1 The routes of Champlain and Brûlé, Dollier and Galinee.

4

But while the men of the North West Company may have thought of building a road north along the Toronto Carrying-Place, it was Chevalier Philippe de Rocheblave, the last British General of Illinois and a man nicknamed the 'farsighted Frenchman', who claimed priority.

De Rocheblave approached Henry Hamilton in 1785 for a tract of land along the Toronto Carrying-Place. This far-sighted man, like so many others of the time, had a dream. He wanted the fur trade, which had previously strewn its wealth along the Ottawa River route, to come to the Toronto area and particularly along the Toronto Carrying-Place from Lake Ontario. His dream was to build a trade centre around the Toronto region where most of the provisions for the voyageurs could be purchased.

De Rocheblave's application was the first to come before Lord Dorchester, then Governor of Quebec (1786-1796).Several weeks after de Rocheblave's request, the North West Company also applied for possession and control of the Grand Portage from Lake Superior to Long Lake, a vital communication link-up with the northwest.

Following the end of the American Rebellion in 1782, the *Treaty of Versailles* posed a serious threat to trade as the British feared that they would have to relinquish hold on their forts at Oswego, Niagara, Detroit and Michilimackinac. The Montreal merchants sent their agents on exploration missions to find an alternative trading route to the north and found the answer to their problems in the discovery of the Toronto Carrying-Place. As an added measure to protect these "pedlars from Quebec", Lord Dorchester "laid before them the proposals for the monopoly of the transportation rights over the Carrying-Place made to him and his Council by the Marquis de Rocheblave, who claimed priority of discovery."[2] The Government favoured de Rocheblave's plan and his application was accepted.

Dorchester was also thinking about a new town which was to have been called Toronto, meaning: "Trees rising out of the water; an opening or gateway into a lake or country; a place of plenty; or a place of many people, or . . . where people meet."[3]

De Rocheblave was determined to have his way. On May 20, 1787, he defined the boundaries of the territory he so badly wanted to acquire and petitioned the government to grant him his precious chunk of land. He staunchly maintained that he was the first person ever to suggest a route northwest of Lake Superior by way of the Carrying-Place, and was quick to point out the advantages of building such a road: He expected to receive his request without any difficulty.

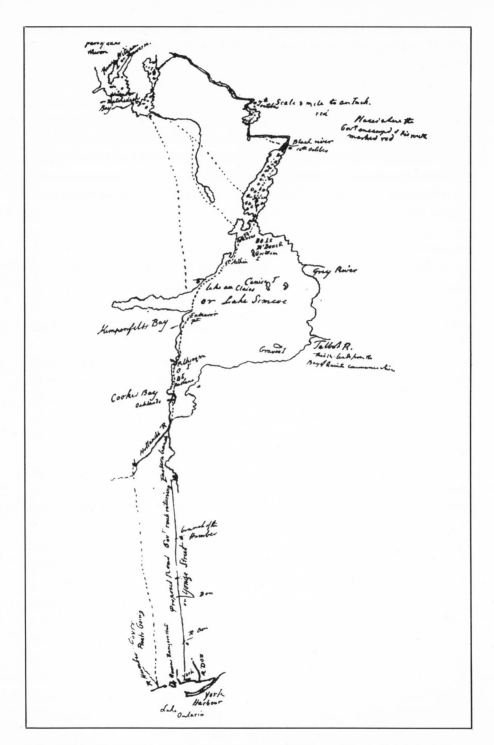

2 One of the earliest known maps of Governor Simcoe's 1793 expedition to Matchedash Bay.

On June 13th he proudly presented Dorchester with his detailed plan for improving the portage route and securing a monopoly of the "carrying rights."

Later, Dorchester wrote a letter to John Collins, the Deputy Surveyor-General who had first surveyed the Toronto Carrying-Place in 1785: "It being thought expedient to join the settlements of the Loyalists near Niagara, to those west of Cataraqui (Fort Frontenac and later Kingston), Sir John Johnson (Superintendant-General of Indian Affairs) has been directed to take such steps with the Indians concerned as may be necessary to establish free and amicable right for government to the interjacent lands not yet purchased on the north of Lake Ontario...as well as to such parts of the country as may be necessary on both sides of the proposed communication from Toronto to Lake Huron." [4]

September 23,1787, an historic meeting took place on the Bay of Quinté near the village of Baskoutiang (a Mississauga name for an old Iroquois village named Quinté), between Collins acting on behalf of the Crown, and three Mississauga Indian chiefs who were eager to trade with the white men.

The agreement that followed became known as the Toronto Purchase, and included the land along the Humber-Holland Trail and the Coldwater Trail, and a tract of land where the future town of Toronto was to be built. The agreement which was ratified at Toronto and partially surveyed on July 7th, 1788, encompassed a rectangular block of land extending 28 miles north and 14 miles east-west.

In August of 1788, surveyor Alexander Aitkin and his party were ready to put the finishing touches on the Toronto Purchase. Among the party was Lord Dorchester, Sir John Johnson, Colonel Butler, (Commander of Butler's Rangers), and an Indian interpreter Nathaniel Lines.

The price paid for the land of the two trails and the proposed townsite was recorded by Nathaniel Lines in his invoice: "Six Bales Strouds, 5 pieces each, 30 pieces; 4 Bales Moltons, each 10 pieces, 40 pieces; 4 keg hoes, 49 each, 196; 8 half-barrels powder; 5 boxes guns; 3 cases shott; 24 brass kettles; 10 kegs of ball; 200lbs. tobacco; 47 carrots; 1 cask containing 3 gro. knives; 10 doz. looking glasses; 4 trunks of linen; 1 hogshead containing 18 pieces of gartering; 24 laced hats; 30 pieces ribbon; 3 gro. fish hooks; 2000 gun flints; 1 box 60 hats; 1 bale flowered flannel, 10 pieces; 5 bales, 3 point blankets, 16 pair each; 1 bale broad cloth, 4 pieces; 5 pieces embossed serge; 1 case barley corn beads; 96 gallons rum, plus 1,700 pounds in cash." [5]

The purchase was made, but de Rocheblave was to see his dream

3 Yonge Street was named after Sir George Yonge, British Secretary of War.

slowly slip away from him. He begged the Government for exclusive privileges along the portage route, plus 1,000 acres at Toronto including the island, and a separate grant of land for his wife and daughter, and 700 acres each for a Captain La Force and Captain Bouchette. But in the end no land was given to de Rocheblave.

John Collins had written on June 10, 1791, to surveyor Augustus Jones stating that Dorchester had already given orders to lay out de Rocheblave's tract of land. Jones, however, did not receive these instructions until a year later, after the arrival of a man who was to become the first Lieutenant-Governor of Upper Canada and was to play a most important part in the development of the road through Ontario woodlands — John Graves Simcoe.

The District Land Board, under whose orders Jones worked, was dissolved by Simcoe's proclamation, and de Rocheblave and his friends did not receive their land.

Discovery of the Don Trail 2

THE TRITON SAILED from Weymouth, England on September 29, 1791, and in the early morning of November 11th, a dignified English gentleman, who had served in the American war, arrived in Canada to take up his position as the first Lieutenant-Governor of Upper Canada.

His name was John Graves Simcoe, an athletic-looking figure who wore the gold-laced uniform of the Queen's Rangers with pride and dignity.

He was a man of action "who lived in times when the rumour of deeds of daring by land and sea were common in all men's mouths."[6]

His rank in the army was Lieutenant-Colonel, conferred upon him a decade earlier.

As early as June 17,1792, Simcoe wrote to his good friend, Sir George Yonge (after whom the great road was to be named), saying that "the military roads and communications will require some investigation and science."[7]

On July 8, 1792, Simcoe took his oath of office. When he made his first visit to the site of Toronto on May 2, 1793, to seek a better military foothold for the capital of his new province, "his attention was . . . occupied with the establishment of a military station at York and the exploration of a route to Lake Huron."[8]

Three months prior to his official installation as Lieutenant-Governor of Upper Canada, Simcoe had recommended the site of London on the Thames River to replace that of Newark (Niagara-on-the-Lake). But Dorchester, who later became the first Lieutenant-Governor of Lower Canada, vetoed Simcoe's choice and ordered him to establish a capital at the Toronto Carrying-Place. Both men were well aware of the possible outbreak of war with the Americans, and both wanted to establish a position of security. Dorchester believed that a naval station on Lake Ontario would provide a stronger defensive base than one that was inland. Simcoe finally agreed that "Toronto appears to be the natural arsenal of Lake Ontario and to afford an easy access overland to Lake Huron."[9]

Simcoe had organized settlers into a militia regiment which he called the Queen's (York) Rangers, the majority of whom were from Butler's Rangers, Sir John Johnson's Regiment, and Jessup's Corps (or the King's Rangers). They had been resettled along the upper St. Lawrence region and Lake Ontario following the American Revolution.

Simcoe too, like de Rocheblave and the men of the North West Company, had a dream. He studied what these men had said about the trail from Lake Ontario to Lake Simcoe and beyond, and had every intention of building a road north to the upper lakes and the northwest.

"I have not as yet been able to cross from Toronto to Lake Huron." said Simcoe in his May 31st, 1793, letter to Alured Clarke (Lieutenant-Governor of Lower Canada 1791-1796), "this I propose to do in the Autumn. But I have good information that a road is very easy to be made to communicate with those waters which fall into Lake Huron. The advantages that may be . . . derived from this communication are of a most extensive nature, and in the present situation of affairs may possibly become of military importance."[10]

About a year after his investiture, Simcoe had his chance to make the trip. At 8 o'clock on July 30, 1793, the topsailed 80-ton schooner called the *Mississauga* arrived in Toronto Harbour. On board was Elizabeth Simcoe, wife of the Lieutenant-Governor, her three children, and a company of Queen's York Rangers. The Governor followed several days later.

Simcoe's new town was christened York on August 27, 1793, in honour of the Duke of York who saved Holland from a French invasion during the French Revolution.

By the fall of 1793, the stage was set for the famed exploration north to Lake Simcoe and the northwest by way of the Humber-Holland Trail. Simcoe no doubt had the dreams of a hero in his mind, but not even he could predict what lay ahead in the coming years, when his new road called Yonge Street would one day become the longest street in the world!

Simcoe's original intention was to make his line of communication into a straight road with townships fronting on it to the east and west. On September 24, 1793, he set out from the town of York, at the mouth of the Humber River, to explore the interior from York to Lake Simcoe and the area of Georgian Bay, and to make his grand dream a reality. It was to prove a more difficult trip than he had bargained for.

His party of explorers included Lieutenant Robert Pilkington of the Royal Engineers, Lieutenant Darling of the 5th Regiment, Lieutenant Givens of the Queen's Rangers, Deputy Provincial Surveyor Alexander Aitkin, Alexander Macdonnell, who kept a diary of the expedition, a group of Indians and a dozen soldiers.

They reached the end of the packhorse route or the end of the Carrying-Place on September 27th, and camped. This was on the north branch of the Holland River. Here, they met a Scottish trader named Cuthbertson, whose hut they had passed the day before at Roches Point on the west side of Cook Bay.

The trail reached a point northwest of the sixth concession of King Township, then etched its way north three-quarters of a mile to the edge of Holland Marsh — "a mere ditch swarming with bullfrogs and water snakes."[11]

The next morning, Simcoe waited while Givens, Aitkin, and three other men went up river to bring back three canoes which had been left for the Governor at the end of the trail above the marsh.

Simcoe's party camped that night on the east bank of the northern branch of the Holland River, on rising ground known as the 'Indian Burying-Ground'. There, they were visited by an Indian Chief known as "The Great Sail" who, as a token of friendship, gave Simcoe a pair of ducks, some beaver meat and a beaver's tail. Simcoe responded by giving the Chief some rum and tobacco.

Journey by water began at the Holland River after all five canoes had been dragged across the marsh.

Well before the white man's arrival in this area, the Indians constructed a pathway or causeway out of tamarack poles through the bush and across the marsh towards the southern branch of the Holland River. The logs were packed lengthwise across the marshy ground and extended to a small pond which flowed into the Holland River.

The paddling procession entered Lake Simcoe in mid-afternoon, September 29th. They passed a Mississauga Indian village at the present site of De Grassi Point (originally known as Oaklands), "then doubled the point, and put in shore in a small bay to dine,"[12] where they were met by a band of Indians. They then set sail after dinner and made their camp in a cedar grove 6 miles from the Indian village

No of lots	Course	Dist	Yonge Street 48 Remarks
			Winds from the N.W. cold, some
			clouds flying –
			Tuesday 25.
			Waiting to get our Bread from
			the Baker – sent David a Mohawk
			to the Grand River – on dispatches
			from the governor – west winds
			pleasant day.
			Wednesday 26th
			recd women of the rangers & issued
			14 days provisions & began my
			survey from a post on the
			bank between 20 & 21, in front
1	N 7° old	8000	At 23°50 All the 1st Concession &c

4 *The first survey of Yonge Street, February, 1794.*

on the Innisfil shore opposite Fox Island.

The next day a strong wind carried them 6 miles further north to Big Bay Point (also known as Point Endeavour) where they put in to have a meal. They then crossed Kempenfelt Bay when it began to rain. Camp was made on the south side of the lake, at an Indian landing-place on the Oro Shore.

On the first day of October they stopped 6 miles further north at Carthew Bay to take further bearings on their direction, and stopped at Francis Island (now Grape Island) where they dined."The Indians used to raise corn upon it, but have not for some time. It is quite covered with long grass."[13]

Shortly after leaving the island, they entered the narrows leading from Lake Simcoe into Lake Couchiching and by sunset the explorers reached the head of the lake, entered the Severn River (also Matchedash River) and encamped.

Macdonnell records the following events: "proceeded down the river, and in the space of two hours had to carry our canoes . . . over two portages. . . Put on shore and dined upon a point where we got various kinds of berries. Mr. Pilkington's canoe and mine, being leaky, were hauled out of the water and gummed well. After dinner pushed off, and about sunset came to the third carrying-place, where, after hauling up our canoes, we encamped. This place is said to be much infested with rattlesnakes; it certainly has much the appearance of it, being almost of solid rock with a few scrubby pines and oaks growing upon it. John Vincall of the Rangers cut one of his toes almost off here."[14]

They crossed the sixth portage the following day and made camp only 2 miles below the last carrying place.

At 11 o'clock in the morning of October 4th, Simcoe and his party entered Matchedash Bay (southern Georgian Bay), after having arrived at the seventh and final portage trail. They sailed across to the opposite shore of Matchedash Bay, "encamped in the woods, a small distance from the lake and about half a mile from Mr. Cowan's house, or rather fort, for it is a square stockade . . . Mr. Cowan is a decent, respectable-looking man and much liked by the Indians. . . He had been settled in Matchedash upwards of fifteen years . . . He makes an annual trip to Michilimackinac to meet his supplies there and forward his furs to Montreal."[15] Cowan lived on a site west of Waubashene and not Fesserton as is often believed.

"I must here observe," said Macdonnell in his diary dated October 5th, "that the Lake Simcoe Indians were much mortified at the Governor not taking the beaver blanket when offered to him."[16]

The next day the party landed on an island called by Cowan *Place la Traverse*, also known as Prince William Henry Island and Beausoleil Island — 6 miles within Matchedash Bay and 9 miles from Cowan's fort.

Near 10 o'clock on the morning of October 6th, 1793, Simcoe and his party left their encampment, launched their canoes, and set off on the return journey home.

In the mid-afternoon on the 11th, they reached the landing place at the Red Pine Fort, so named because of the red pine trees that covered the surrounding hills. It was a log building with shutters, and was later renamed Gwillimbury by Simcoe. The Red Pine Fort landing was also known by several other names: The Landing at The Pine Fort,

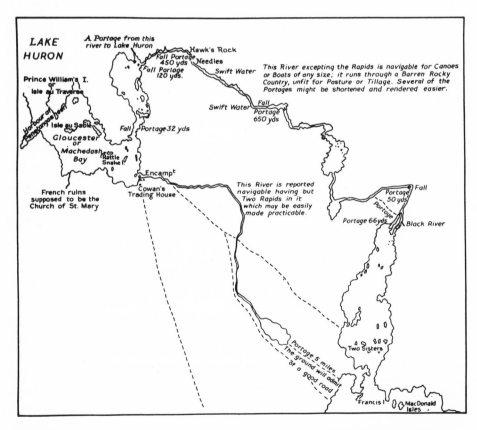

5 *Map showing northern route of Simcoe's expedition to Matchedash Bay in 1793.*

Holland Landing (after Surveyor-General Holland), Canoe Landing, Soldier's Landing, the Steamboat Landing and the Lower Landing. Military and naval provisions and presents for Indians were often deposited here. It was also a place often visited by many early travellers like Sir John Franklin who left from there in 1825 on his first overland expedition to the Arctic Seas, and by John Galt en route to Goderich by way of Penetanguishene. Indians and fur traders often camped in the open space near the landing, where as many as 30 wigwams clustered together.

A mile-and-a-half north of Red Pine Fort was the Upper Landing, often referred to as Johnson's Landing, named after its first settler Joseph Johnson Senior. The Upper Landing was an ancient place of embarkation for Indian war parties and hunting parties, and was also used for canoes and lighter craft which could get higher up the stream than the Lower Landing.

Simcoe was determined to follow a different path home, but this put the expedition in grave difficulty. Provisions were extremely low and it had become imperative that Macdonnell, Givens and Givens' servant remain behind at the Carrying-Place with John Vincall, who had cut his toe on October 2nd. They would remain behind and live off a meagre supply of food until a horse could be sent from York for Vincall to ride back on. It was October 11th.

Simcoe and his staff, Alexander Aitkin, his survey crew and a few Indians set out to find their way to York by the new route. Simcoe followed a course from the east branch of the Holland River, while Macdonnell returned to York, some time later, by the western route to the mouth of the Humber River. The ironic part about this is that Macdonnell the diarist was not present for what turned out to be the first known journey down Yonge Street!

Instead Aitkin, who also kept a diary, recorded the journey south to York with Simcoe.

With the onslaught of a heavy rain storm on October 11th, Simcoe's party was forced to camp in a cedar swamp on the east branch of the Holland River.

They lost their way several times after setting out on the 12th, and breakfasted a mile south of Armitage on the east branch of the Humber River. They regained the trail once more — a trail which would soon be gouged into a wagon road by early settlers.

Simcoe still believed them to be lost on the 13th, and feared the worst as only one day's rations were left.

6 Mrs. Elizabeth Simcoe.

7 John Graves Simcoe.

However, they came upon a surveyor's line at the fourth concession line from the Bay, at what is now Eglinton Avenue. Augustus Jones had come upon the Humber-Holland Trail a year before while surveying in the area, and it was probably his survey line that the party crossed.

The last bits of food were eaten for breakfast about a mile-and-a-half on the trail from York. Shortly before 3 o'clock in the afternoon of October 14th, Simcoe and his expedition reached the camp on Garrison Creek opposite Old Fort York.

During the next several days, Aitkin was busy at work drawing maps and plans of Simcoe's new route from York to Lake Huron and back again along the Don Trail.

Macdonnell's vigil was cold, wet and exhausting. Marsh hens, ducks and Indian corn were used as food, the latter being pounded and boiled for breakfast. Birch bark was collected to make spears with which to catch fish.

Macdonnell and Givens made their way back to the Indian village at De Grassi Point to get more supplies while Vincall and Givens' servant remained behind. "It beginning to rain and the wind shifting suddenly . . . we were forced to carry our canoe . . . to the opposite side of the fire, and turned our backs to the lake. Crept under the canoe and passed a very uncomfortable night."[17]

Two days later, Macdonnell and Givens made their way back to the Carrying-Place, though both men were ill.

They eventually arrived near the end of the Carrying-Place, and met Cuthbertson who gave them some chocolate and a gallon of liquor.

"Soon after encamping . . . Sergeant Malley and another man of the Rangers . . . arrived from York with a horse for the lame man. The Governor was pleased to send us, by them, brandy, wine, tea, sugar, pork, and bread . . . and concluding the day with a can of grog to his health, went to bed."[18]

Having been away for twenty-seven days, Macdonnell and his men arrived back at York on October 20th.

So convinced was Simcoe of the advantages of the new route in spite of the difficulties he had encountered, that within a week of his return from Matchedash Bay, October 19 he wrote to Henry Dundas, Secretary for the Colonies, saying that he had "ascertained by a route hitherto unknown but to some Indian hunters, that there is an easy portage between York and the waters which fall into Lake Huron of not more than thirty miles in extent, and through a country perfectly calculated for agricultural purposes."[19] His plan was to have it surveyed in the following spring, with the hope that his new military street would be completed the ensuing autumn.

Augustus Jones met with Governor Simcoe on February 23, 1794, three days before he was to begin the official survey of the new route. Jones received a sketch prepared by Lieutenant Robert Pilkington and one by Alexander Aitkin showing the proposed course of the new road. Pilkington's map was probably entitled "sketch of a route from York Town on Lake Ontario to the Harbour of Penetanguishene on Lake Huron in Upper Canada, by Lt. Pilkington Rl. Engrs. in the year 1793."[20] Unfortunately, like so many other documents, this map has been lost or destroyed. Writers generally agree that Mrs. Simcoe made a tracing of the original map, usually accredited to Pilkington. This was probably the same map Mrs. Simcoe referred to in her diary for the date of October 25, 1793, when she wrote to her correspondent in England "I send a map to elucidate the Governor's journey . . . The western side of the lake is drawn from Mr. Pilkington's sketches, the eastern from other accounts."[21]

Mrs. Simcoe's sketch also differs from the map made in 1817, which was a copy of the original, and was for many years the only map of Simcoe's trip until the tissue paper tracing was discovered by Willoughby Cole, the great-grandson of Simcoe himself.

Attached to the route from Holland Landing to York, Mrs. Simcoe's map had a note that read "Proposed Road or Yonge Street, Governor's route returning."[22] Despite several errors made by the original map makers, there is also a pencil line on the tissue paper sketch, drawn to show that there was the intention of making use of the little-known trail from Orillia to Matchedash Bay (which afterwards became the Coldwater Road); this route was also to be called Yonge Street.

If this notation was made by Mrs. Simcoe in October, 1793, then it would be the first known indication that the new road through the woods from York to the Upper Lakes was to be called Yonge Street.

The great road north was to be named after Sir George Yonge, Secretary of War in the British Cabinet from 1782 to 1794, and a member of Parliament for Honiton in the county of Devon. Yonge was also a member of the Royal Society of Antiquaries and an authority on Roman roads in Britain. He held the offices of Vice-Treasurer of Ireland and Master of the Mint. He died in 1812, never having set foot on Canadian soil despite the fact that his very good friend John Graves Simcoe ruled the land.

Yonge Street was not the first highway built by Simcoe. Having initially wanted his capital to be at London on the Thames River, he began construction in September, 1793, of a road west of the river and named it Dundas Street after the Secretary for the Colonies.

After his difficult journey to Georgian Bay via the Humber-Holland Trail, Simcoe rejected the idea of building a straight road between the Humber River and the west branch of the Holland River and ordered a survey of a straight road following the Don Trail - the "new route" he had followed back to York. It was the least-known trail in the area and was probably used mostly by the Mississauga Indians.

Simcoe and his expedition may very well have been the first men to follow the entire length of the Don Trail which extended to Lake Ontario; and Simcoe may have been the last man of importance to have used the Humber-Holland route as well.

Earlier, rich schools of salmon had attracted Huron Indians to the area, and Iroquois war parties and Jesuit missionaries had probably followed the Don Trail. Now it was to take on a new significance because it was along this trail that Yonge Street was to be built.

Augustus Jones on February 26th, 1794, began his first official survey of Yonge Street. He took four Rangers to help him and carried 14 days' worth of provisions. The party returned home on March 19th.

During the survey, Jones and his party had missed the Landing at the Pine Fort by about a mile very close to the Upper Landing. The error made it necessary to resurvey the entire line again, but this time they began near the site of Ellenholme, an old house on the west side of Yonge Street about a mile north of the village of Holland Landing, or the Lower Landing. Near the back of the house in a deep gulley by the Holland River was the Old Indian Landing, or the Upper Canoe Landing.

The Mississauga Indians of De Grassi Point didn't like what Jones was trying to do because they believed that this particular region through which upper Yonge Street was to run had not been included in the land purchase of 1788. They were right; the trail crossed the northern boundary of the Toronto Purchase, 8½ miles east of the western boundary of the County of York. The Indians were well within their claim and threatened to cause trouble. But luckily for Jones there was an Indian Chief with the expedition who explained to the Indians that the running of the line did not mean taking the land away from them.

Jones later married the daughter of the noted Mohawk warrior, Terrihogah.

The southern part of the survey began on March 13th from a point about one mile north of the Lower Landing or half a mile south of the Upper Canoe Landing.

The winter up to this time had been a very mild one, despite the odd snowfall and case of frostbite. The weather was well suited for surveying as there were no leaves on the trees to block the surveyor's view along the trail.

The hard forest ground made the survey an easy task. The forest was open and relatively uncluttered; the underbrush was thin; and few obstacles hindered the work at hand. The soldiers of the Queen's Rangers acted as axemen and sliced away at what bushes there were.

The general course of Yonge Street had now been laid out, but there still remained a more detailed job of surveying which included measuring the street and marking the lots.

At the beginning of April, 1794, Acting Surveyor-General D.W. Smith wrote to Augustus Jones: "Should the road from York to Matchedash be surveyed and fixed upon, it is His Excellency the Lieut. Governor's wish that you lay out the lots in two hundred acres . . ."[23]

April 25th Smith wrote to Aitkin, directing him to make a survey along the line run by Jones and to lay off on each side of the survey line a "road which is to be a chain (about 66-feet) wide, lots of 20 chains wide fronting on the road and . . . containing 200 acres more or less . . ."[24] Lots were to be numbered from one upwards on each side of the road.

In May, 1794, Alexander Aitkin and a group of Queen's Rangers worked side by side in laying out lots, from the present site of Eglinton Avenue to Holland Landing. Yonge Street lots on either side of Concession 1 numbered continuously from no. 1 at present-day Eglinton Avenue to no. 133 at the mouth of the Holland River. Oak Ridges at Bond Lake, for example, would be considered as Whitchurch Township, Concession 1, lot no. 63.

By the end of May Yonge Street had been opened only as far north as lot no. 17 or a quarter-of-a-mile north from what is now Sheppard Avenue: opening a road meant that a path 20-feet wide had been cleared through the woods.

When Jones reached York Mills he was confronted by a swampy marshland and was forced to cut the road to the east, down the side of the ravine, following the contour of the land rather than cutting a line straight down the hill at York Mills as he originally intended. There was no problem crossing the small river bed, but Jones was faced with a dilemma when he cut his way up the very steep incline of the ravine on the north side of the Don River, now known as Old Yonge Street. Once the road had reached the top of the hill, it followed the edge of the ravine back to the line originally laid out on the map for Yonge Street. This was one of many detours the early surveyors were forced to make.

Also, before the month of May was over, 4 miles of usable road had been cleared north of Eglinton.

Simcoe's plans were interrupted that August when a disturbance in the Detroit area forced him to withdraw his troops from road duty and order them to the Niagara frontier to protect the border against a possible American attack on Canada. The work on Yonge Street temporarily ground to a halt.

By August, Yonge Street extended to lot no. 29, a quarter-of-a-mile south of Thornhill. Trees had been chopped down and several bridges had been built, but the great road was not progressing as rapidly as Simcoe would have liked.

Therefore, in September, the Governor selected an alternative plan for the building of the road, which included a man named William Von Berczy whose name would eventually become known throughout the town of York and Upper Canada.

William Von Berczy's Problem   3

EARLY IN THE SUMMER of 1794, a fleet of small vessels glided swiftly and quietly through the waters of Lake Ontario to the mouth of the Don River. They were vessels with a cargo of livestock, building implements and supplies, equipment to build sawmills and gristmills — and 64 German families who had been smuggled into the country.

William Von Berczy had hired fifteen boats, manned with armed oarsmen and Indians, and had enticed the German families into Upper Canada with promises of free land, employment and the opportunity for a happy life.

Besides being a painter, architect, engineer and active business-man who had come to North America to make his fortune in land dealings, Berczy was also the colonization agent and Canadian director in Upper Canada for the German Land Company. This was an American operation based in New York in which the Vice-President of the United States, Aaron Burr, held an active interest.

In 1792, Berczy had guided his German settlers from Hamburg to the Pultney Settlement in the Genesee Valley of New York State. After the American Revolution, promoters on both sides of the Atlantic had bought thousands of acres of land at great discounts from the poverty-stricken American states, and land companies sought out future colonists from war-torn Germany to come to America. Theoreti-cally through settlement the land value would increase sharply, and thus help get the country back on its feet. But the Genesee Valley Settlement was a failure and Berczy looked to Upper Canada as a last resort to help save his people.

Even as early as 1792, Simcoe was offering free grants of land to every family and settler; and no doubt this was a major reason for Berczy's decision to come to Upper Canada.

The arrival could have been mutually rewarding for Berczy and Simcoe. Berczy needed land and he was known to have road-building skills which Simcoe required, Yonge Street at that time still being only a path through the woods along which no wagon could travel.

Aitkin, by May, 1794, had already laid out lots of land on Yonge Street as far north as Holland Landing, but a Sergeant Pearce with a company of Queen's Rangers had cut the road only as far as Thornhill, and even this stretch of road was still in poor condition.

Berczy agreed to build and finish a wagon road from York to Holland Landing in one year's time for the price of four choice lots on Yonge Street by the Don River in Thornhill: "Nearly midway on Yonge Street between Lake Ontario and Gwillimbury (Holland Landing), the Provincial Government had reserved four lots of two hundred acres each, situated equally on both sides of the road, through which the river Don runs, to be sold for raising a fund to be employed towards the making of Yonge Street a practicable road for wagons. These four lots he offered to me for this purpose."[25] Berczy's plan was to capitalize on future land sales.

But Berczy was not satisfied that the four lots in question would entirely pay for the expense of opening the whole road. The Queen's Rangers by that time had only cut down the trees in the line surveyed by Augustus Jones during the previous winter.

With the German families waiting to be placed on farm lots in the new country, Berczy petitioned the Simcoe Government for one million acres of land, for what he called "settlement promotion". This was in March of 1794. He confronted Simcoe again in May for his 1 million acres, but his German Land Company received only 64,000 acres in Markham Township, 17 miles north of York (Toronto). The initial grant was considered much too high for any one person or company. Berczy accepted the offer with the condition that he receive more land should he and his associates prove their ability in supporting their people.

Berczy was willing and eager to enter into such an arrangement and finish Yonge Street so that a cart could pass easily and safely, "provided it shall not come to a great expense . . . I wish to do it in such a manner that the Government and the public shall be fully satisfied."[26]

Berczy said, "I determined immediately to cut through the woods at my own expense (from lot no. 29 to Holland Landing, about seven-and-a-half miles north of lot no. 1 at Eglinton Avenue) a sufficiently large and comfortable road for the passage of wagons, for a distance of about 30 miles through the lands laid out for my first settlement, with all the necessary bridges over the waters which I should find in my way."[27]

The road from the town of York to lot no. 29 had already been opened, but because of the many hills, horses and cattle passed with great difficulty over this stretch. The high muddy river banks made it necessary to build bridges over the creeks. In essence, Berczy was under contract to finish that part of the road already opened from York to lot no. 29, and to construct and open the road from that point to Holland Landing.

Originally Berczy's men, under the direction of Philip Eckardt, cut a rough trail up Yonge Street to the present site of Thornhill along what is now highway no. 7, through the land laid out for his first settlement.

When he first arrived in York, Berczy's land in Markham had not yet been surveyed and this was to cause him considerable problems. Abraham Iredell finally began the survey in mid-September of 1794 and finished it at the end of October.

Berczy came down with malaria in August and was still ill at the beginning of September when so many things had yet to be done. But despite this, Berczy approached his duties with enthusiasm and as much energy as he could muster. For weeks he pleaded with the Government for surveys and clear instructions relating directly to the "Yonge Street job," which he had promised to complete as far north as Holland Landing within one year. He did his best to convince his troupe to follow him, and every second day while he was ill enquired about surveyors and surveys.

After recovering from his illness, Berczy spent several days in mid-September at the townsite of York and on Yonge Street supervising the cutting out of the road through the bush.

At the beginning of September he sent three dozen of his settlers along with sixty hired axemen to begin work on Yonge Street, and clear out part of the lot where York was to be built. But since Berczy's own land had not yet been surveyed, he could not begin his contracted work on Yonge Street to Holland Landing until the very end of October when Iredell completed his work.

During this annoying delay, Berczy began building his own house and storehouse in York and he found employment for some of his men in clearing part of the ground at York set aside for the township.

"Having a great many hired hands for my buildings, I have already given orders to a part to open part of the road from Johnson's (at lot no. 29) to the little lake (Bond Lake at lot no. 63, a distance of about eight-and-a-half miles) till I can come there myself."[28]

At least one hundred oxen worked on the southern portion of Yonge Street and on the barren townsite of York. As the work progressed, some eighty cows, heifers, and steers were driven to Asa Johnson's farm at lot no. 29 on Yonge Street, and some cows were sent to the home of Nicholas Miller at lot no. 34, where they were distributed individually to Berczy's settlers. The remaining oxen continued to clear, flatten and "bulldoze" Yonge Street and other pioneer roads. They also hauled logs and barrels of food to the various building sites of the German Land Company.

In a letter to Surveyor David Smith, November 30, 1794, Berczy indicated that he had only finished Yonge Street as far north as

8 The first Yonge Street tollgate, just north of Bloor Street, 1830.

lot no. 36, only about one third of the way to Holland Landing, but promised that as soon as he had made the necessary arrangements he would continue to work on the road. He hoped that at least by the spring of 1795, Yonge Street would be completely finished from York to Johnson's farm at lot no. 29; and that "the piece of Yonge Street from no. 29 to River Holland . . . shall be performed as good as circumstances will possibly admit."[29]

Berczy had built more than 45 miles of good wagon roads, including those in his settlement area; and by the end of November of 1794 he had settled 78 families.

Iredell gave Berczy a draft of his partial survey made in the Markham area, and between the end of October and the middle of November Berczy and his axemen, along with their stalwart teams of oxen, cleared settlement roads into their land.

It was only during the early winter season of 1794 that Berczy could show the German settlers the exact location of their new homes. Forty houses had previously been built but they were mere huts, erected quickly as temporary dwellings.

"Snow lay deep on the ground and the German families trudged north along the bed of a frozen stream to begin life on their farms in a roofless wilderness."[30]

Four Markham pioneers left their huts in January, 1795, to work on Yonge Street; and by February, twelve of Berczy's German settlers and nine hired axemen were at work on the great road.

The road workers earned between 5 and 6 shillings per day including meals and drinks worth about 1 shilling.

The oxen were invaluable. They could haul four barrels of provisions weighing as much as nine hundred pounds over the hills and dales of Yonge Street. Two teams of four oxen each were employed for five days, bringing needed provisions from York.

Berczy estimated that 98 acres of ground area had been cleared. This included 15 miles of Yonge Street which was 18-feet wide and 30 miles of road in his Markham settlement. This cost him 147 pounds, or just under $600, plus the cost of food rations and the necessary bridges. The main reason for such a low cost was that the settlers themselves assisted and worked at a very modest rate.

There was Isaac Devins, who also helped Berczy with the great road. He was constable of the Humber, a foreman on Yonge Street, and leader of one of Berczy's roadbuilding teams in February of 1795.

There was Asa Johnson, the first official settler on Yonge Street who, because he owned oxen, worked for Berczy on the construction.

There were men like William Cooper, Stephen Colby and Richard Lawrence who were once inhabitants of the town of York and now settlers on Yonge Street. They worked as "tinker - carpenters in the town and then as pioneer bushbeaters in the country."

There were also explorers and speculative settlers among Berczy's hired help who begged him to locate or settle them on choice parcels of land. Once they had a look at the countryside along the Yonge Street area, they knew it was to their advantage to settle along the great road. They also knew that Berczy had the authority to direct applicants for land to the still-undesignated lots on Yonge Street.

9 *The Queen's Rangers under Lieutenant-Governor Simcoe, cutting out Yonge Street, 1795.*

Despite his illness, the cold weather and poor communication with the acting surveyor, despite the problems of feeding and providing shelters for his people and facing the monumental task of building colonization roads through the woods to his land, Berczy somehow found the time to become interested and involved with yet another scheme. In the late autumn of 1794, Berczy switched his interest to the possibility of building a canal between the Rouge and Holland Rivers. Having explored the country for some weeks, Berczy believed that such a canal would provide a shorter route to the north for the fur trade business, shortening the portage route from Lake Ontario to Lake Huron. He enthused: "By an easy water communication, goods might be carried in boats from Lake Ontario without unloading . . . a method of conveying goods to and from the northwest, greatly more advantageous than the transport over Yonge Street as proposed by Mr. de Rocheblave."[31]

Berczy also thought the canal would entice traders to cross Markham diagonally, bringing prosperity and the potential for stimulating trade to his settlers in the area.

Simcoe encouraged Berczy to develop the idea for a canal and explore the area: he envisioned a harbour and landing at the mouth of the Rouge River and reserved the land for himself and the government. Both men agreed to continue this project in the spring of 1795; and in the early summer Berczy began to clear the channel of the stream. For the moment, Simcoe's plans for Yonge Street came to a halt.

Berczy, however, was doomed to failure. The seeds of destruction were planted in November, 1794, when he first became interested in the Rouge Canal project, for this was the beginning of several conflicts that spelled the end of his work, his four Thornhill lots, the German Town site of Richmond Hill, and the Markham lands he had worked so hard to get.

Berczy's fatal waterway project indirectly retarded the settlement of Yonge Street because money and time were spent on the Rouge River project instead of on Yonge Street. Berczy's workers became ill, and some had been injured on the job. It had been impossible to plant crops because of the lateness of the season, and so he found he had to care for his people for an additional twelve months. "All the embarrassing circumstances, unforeseen and inevitable losses, caused partly by the appearance of a war between Great Britain and the United States and partly by natural events, produced the aggravating

10 William Von Berczy, self-portrait.

11 Sir John Franklin.

effect of increasing the expenses till now, to the amount of 45,000 dollars."[32]

The failure of the crops in 1795 and the subsequent famine put a further damper on Berczy's hopes as the flow of supplies and money ended. With only meagre rations of potatoes and turnips, Berczy had to request food from the Queen's Rangers. The people of the German Land Company were disillusioned by the high development costs of the venture and the great delay in obtaining patents for the granted townships, and the company was unable to proceed as planned.

Berczy was to have completed Yonge Street from York to Holland Landing but he had only built that portion of the road from lot no. 29 below Thornhill to lot no. 35 where the road turned off at Langstaff. On May 28, 1795, Peter Russell, Chairman of the Executive Council and the man who was to succeed Simcoe as Administrator of Upper Canada, wrote a letter to the Governor recommending that Berczy's claim to the four lots be forfeited because he had not completed his contract within the allowable time.

The German Land Company as well, came under the scrutinizing eye of the Canadian Government, which became apprehensive of the company's foreign background and grasp of the initial undertaking. Berczy's settlers were considered aliens who could neither be trusted nor legally own land before seven years' residence in York as subjects of the Crown. Berczy's own insatiable ambition for land, power and wealth also caused concern.

As a result, the Canadian authorities refused to grant Berczy and his settlers the deeds in Markham on the grounds that the people were unnaturalized immigrants who would have to wait for a number of years before they could become citizens. The Executive Council declared that Berczy had justly forfeited his promised lots of land, but recommended that he be granted land elsewhere as compensation.

The Yonge Street lots reverted back to the Crown and other lands promised to Berczy at the mouth of the Rouge River were turned over to government office holders. Berczy's own grant of land in Markham had not been officially surveyed when the first agreement regarding the road was drawn up, and consequently he could not receive title to his property.

In 1796, Simcoe's health began to deteriorate and he left Canada on July 21st. He died at Exeter in England and was buried in the chapel at Wolford on the night of November 4, 1806. Simcoe's

33

successor, Peter Russell, who acted as Administrator of Upper Canada, did not fulfill the promise Simcoe had made to William Von Berczy.

Berczy had erected the first sawmill and gristmill in the part of York known as the German Mills, where farmers from as far away as Belleville and the Head of the Lake brought their grain. This was one of the most productive farming districts in all of Ontario at the time. But they were advertised for sale in 1805 to help pay Berczy's debts. He left for Montreal, a ruined and embittered man. From 1804 to 1813 he worked as a portrait painter until his mysterious death in New York. His family thought the body had disappeared, but found his coffin in a New York churchyard — a coffin filled with rocks.

Determined not to let his Yonge Street dream die because of Berczy's failure, Simcoe, before his departure from Canada, made preparations for another survey of the road and further construction.

David Smith, Acting Surveyor-General of the Province, received a letter on Christmas Eve, 1795, from Augustus Jones : "His Excellency was pleased to direct me, previous to my surveying the township of York, to proceed on Yonge Street, to survey and open a cart road from the harbour at York to Lake Simcoe."[33] Four days later, 30 Queen's Rangers were assigned to accompany Jones on his journey.

Jones began his survey on January 4, 1796, from a post he had previously imbedded on the bank of Lake Ontario by York Harbour. He and his survey party reached the Landing on February 16th — an expedition lasting forty-three days. The distance of the survey, according to Jones' notebook and diary, was 34 miles and 53 chains (1 chain equals 66-feet), from York to a "pine tree marked at landing; timber, yellow and white pines; sandy soil; slight winds from the north; cloudy, cold weather."[34] Some sources suggest that this distance was a mile less than Jones indicated in his diary — a document which has since been lost. It is quite possible that he ended his survey at the same point he began the survey in 1794, about one mile north of the Lower Landing or just south of the Upper Landing. This would account for the mile difference in the length of the survey.

February 16th, Jones and his party began the return journey to York, and on February 20th, Jones went to the Garrison at York and waited to see Governor Simcoe and "informed him that Yonge Street is opened from York to the Pine Fort Landing, Lake Simcoe."[35]

The First Settlers 4

T HE SETTLERS BEGAN to head up the great road to meet the challenge of the trees, swamps, marshlands and cruel winters.

As they settled in their isolated cabins, far from the water, they soon had to make their own paths through the woods — paths that widened for horsemen and later for vehicles.

Settlement was thinly dispersed over hundreds of miles; the land was heavily wooded with many streams, and the freezing and thawing conditions made the task difficult. Once the road was cut through the mud and bush it had to be straightened and graded; hills needed levelling and bridges had to be built.

Those who populated the new land were the English, the French Huguenots from New Jersey, English Quakers and Puritans. Pennsylvania Dutch made up the largest group — most of them were Germans from New York; others originated from the German section of Switzerland. Because the Americans couldn't pronounce the word 'Deutsch' for German, they called them 'Dutch'.

Other pioneers in the new land were Mennonites, Lutherans, Methodists, Baptists and Presbyterians. They too, Like Berczy's people, were brought to Upper Canada by promises of free land.

At the same time, there was a growing concern in Upper Canada over the ever-increasing number of American settlers, who in the first decade of the nineteenth century more than doubled the population. Rumours that the Americans along Yonge Street had no respect for the Canadian Government troubled the political leaders of the day.

The American settlers came to Canada in covered wagons pulled by oxen, bringing with them their horses, cattle and building equipment. Some travelled only 8 miles a day over a distance of 500 miles around Lake Erie and across Niagara.

The first English-speaking settlers were the United Empire Loyalists who came to Canada with nothing but the clothes on their backs. Many remained encamped in their tents while surveyors completed the division of lots; others had to sleep under trees.

From Genesee, New York, came Nicholas Miller who called himself the first settler on Yonge Street. He eventually took up residence on the east side of Yonge Street in Markham Township. He was brought to Canada by Simcoe to build a government sawmill on the Humber River. With him came his wife, several friends, and his personal belongings. The Millers literally dug their way out of the wilderness and built a homestead for themselves.

In the spring of 1793, there were only Indians living in the area and Yonge Street had not even been surveyed. The first official survey wasn't begun until February, 1794, by Jones and lots weren't laid out until May, 1794, by Aitkin and Jones. The Millers weren't officially assigned to their lot until September of that year, and lost the distinction of being first because of this technicality.

Asa Johnson who built the first log house east of Yonge Street in the Township of Vaughn was acknowledged in 1795 as being the first settler on Yonge Street, and thus the Millers had to settle for second place.

When Mrs. Johnson petitioned the government for land in 1794 for herself and her two youngest sons, she wrote that her family was among the "first to undertake the fatigue of going into the woods on Yonge Street." [36]

Yonge Street was a narrow, twisting trail dotted with ugly tree stumps and treacherous holes with steep hills and unbridged streams; broad tree branches were fastened to wagon wheels to prevent the wagons from rolling down steep hills or sinking into the mud; other travellers had to remove the wheels altogether and float them across the Don River like boats.

Bears and wolves proved to be troublesome and a bounty was offered for their heads.

The Ketchum family journeyed on foot from Columbia County in the Catskills to Oswego, and then by boat to Upper Canada. Jesse Ketchum made a fortune in the tanning business; his elder brother, Seneca, was the leading figure in the founding of St. John's, York Mills — an early place of worship of the Church of England, and an outpost of the mission at York.

The Mercer family drove from Pennsylvania in 1794 in a wagon with a cow tied behind. Mercer was an Irishman who cleared farmland near the top of the Yonge Street hill in the area of York Mills.

Cornelius Anderson, a Scotsman who was disbanded from his British regiment in New Brunswick following the American Revolution, settled with his wife and nine children on the west side of Yonge Street north of the Don River.

Cornelius Van Nostrand, who once held a commission in the British Army, brought his family from Oyster Bay, Long Island, to a farm on Yonge Street in 1800 to open a general store.

"The road is as yet very bad; there are pools of water among the roots of trees and fallen logs in swampy spots, and these pools, being half frozen, render them still more disagreeable when the horses plunge into them."[37]

The Indians also gave cause for worry, because of their resentment of the invasion of their hunting grounds by the white men. Relations with the Indians soon improved, however, and the farm of Jacob Munshaw in Vaughn Township became one of the Indians' favourite camping spots on journeys up and down Yonge Street. With their heads decorated with eagle plumes and war spears in their hands, they travelled down Yonge Street to collect their yearly bounty.

On the tombstone of Mrs. Elizabeth Cummer and Mrs. Eva Cober, both daughters of Jacob Fisher, who came to Upper Canada with their parents in 1796, is the statement: "of the first settlers on Yonge Street, they were the fifth family."[38]

In 1793, roads were placed under the scrutiny of Overseers who were elected at public meetings. They had to supervise all construction and repair work for a certain section of the road. The law required all men living in townships to contribute up to 12 days free labour on the roads each year. This was the beginning of statute labour.

Also appointed were Fence Viewers and Pathmasters: Nicholas Miller in 1797, was elected Overseer of Highways and Fence Viewer for a section of Yonge Street. Fences had to be five-feet high with no space through the fence of more than four-inches. Hogs under three months old were allowed to run at large in the country without yokes, but all hogs running around in the town of York had to be yoked and ringed to the nose. If the owner failed to do so, his hog would be impounded until he paid one dollar for its release.

People were also prosecuted for obstructing the streets with piles of wood and stone, or for digging pits in the road.

The basic land allotment to each settler was 200 acres. Those who received this land had to perform settlement duties: the first task was to build a house on their lot within one year. Trees had to be cut down, logs and bush had to be burned, and tree stumps on the road had to be cut low enough to allow a wagon to pass over them. Five acres in every 100 had to be fenced in and cleared within one year, and the settler also had to construct a quarter mile stretch of road in front of his property.

Under the supervision of Pathmasters, the adult male settlers were required to work on roads for a certain number of days each year. They used their own tools and provided oxen if they had any. Those who didn't work the required number of days were fined, but with the severity of the work that faced them it was incredibly difficult to fulfill their statute labour obligations.

A period of seven years was allowed to complete settlement duties. The owner then received a deed for his land. Otherwise, the land reverted to the Crown.

Preference was given to United Empire Loyalists, their children, and former military personnel who received grants of as much as 1,200 acres of land, without having to pay an administrative fee or fulfill settlement duties.

Persons fulfilling their annual quota of statute labour would not have to do emergency work should the road cave in after it was finished.

It was quite usual for the roadbuilders of the day to leave the stumps of trees in the road until they had rotted. Sometimes they would return to clear away the debris, but not often enough.

In 1800, a Stump Act was put into force in York; such a law being in existence in Vermont at the time. It was proclaimed that each drunk was forced to remove at least one stump from the streets.

When a road was opened, two surveyors with compasses would follow the lone explorer. Trees were notched, indicating the boundary of the road and woodmen chopped down any trees in the course of the proposed roadway. Men followed behind to clear away tree trunks and brush; and at the rear of the building team were the wagons hauling provisions for the men.

A group of 15 aristocratic French Royalists and their following of 41 Frenchmen led by General Joseph Genèvieve Count de Puisaye, a high-ranking officer in Louis XVI's army, settled in Upper Canada from 1789 - 1799 to form a military station.

This was the first settlement *en masse* up Yonge Street. They were French refugees who had lost their land during the French Revolution. Known as the Puisaye Settlement, their townsite in Windham in the area of Oak Ridges ran north for 11 lots on either side of Yonge Street.

Simcoe wanted this northern settlement to provide a military safeguard for his young capital in the event of an attack from the north.

Captain William Graham, Justice of the Peace in the township of Whitchurch, wrote to de Puisaye complaining about the condition of Yonge Street to the south: "All the people in my neighbourhood have been making . . . grievous complaints . . . about shutting up the road so as (one) cannot go (a) mile (or) two with their teams. I must beg . . . you to order your people to clear the logs and brush out of the roads that they have cut into it (Yonge Street). " [39]

The French noblemen and their retainers who settled in the wilderness were not properly equipped for the hard work of clearing the land and road construction, and the Puisaye settlement failed completely.

The settlers sold their land and moved elsewhere. De Puisaye abandoned the project, deciding that Yonge Street was impossible for transportation, and left the country for England.

Surveyor-General D.W. Smith was determined that a report should be drawn up showing how the settlement duties had been performed on Yonge Street. John Stegman, an officer who had fought for Britain in the American Revolution and had come to Upper Canada to seek his fortune after the war, was given the task of performing this investigation. On June 10, 1801, Stegman reported "that from the town of York to the three mile post (on Poplar Plains Road south of St. Clair Avenue), the road is cut, and that as yet, the greater part of the said distance is not passable for any carriage whatever on account of logs which lie in the street; from thence to lot 1 on Yonge Street (Eglinton Avenue), the road is very narrow and difficult to pass at any time." [40]

Certain parts of the road were in only fair condition while other sections were intolerable. The road north of Aurora in the district just being opened by the Quakers was not complete, although the newcomers appeared to be working on the road in several places.

In his summary, Stegman criticized the French settlers who had

12 *William Lyon Mackenzie.*

13 *The John Thompson omnibus.*

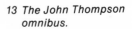

14 *William Botsford Jarvis, Sheriff of
    the Home District in York.*

15 *The William Weller Stage Line, 1830.*

41

lived on Yonge Street several years before and cited them for being most neglectful in the clearing of the street.

But it was not only the northern sections that were in disrepair. In 1796, when York was a town of some twelve city blocks, Berczy and his men had extended the street south to the present location of Yorkville Avenue, just north of Bloor Street, but the section below Yorkville soon fell into disuse.

At its southern end, Yonge Street was separated from the centre of town and the market place by a large swamp. Those who laid out the area of the new town did not expect the street to extend directly to the water's edge of Lake Ontario. In the original plans, Yonge Street stopped just short of Lot Street, later renamed Queen Street. This section of the road from Queen Street north to Yorkville was narrow, neglected and full of ugly stumps, dotted with windfalls and lacking grading and bridges; it was referred to as "the road to Yonge Street". The area south of Queen Street was privately owned land; and when the new town was laid out in 1797, no provision was made for extending Yonge Street south of Queen Street.

All traffic travelling south into the town had to detour to the east of Yonge Street along Toronto Street, one block east of Yonge. When travelling south of Queen Street it was necessary to continue to the east of Yonge Street to avoid private property such as the tan yard owned by Jesse Ketchum. Farmers from the north turned off Yonge Street at Yorkville and proceeded south in a haphazard fashion across vacant private property. Later, those who owned this land were given other lots in exchange for the right of way through their property.

A public meeting was held to discuss the idea of making the direct approach to York more available. The *Upper Canada Gazette* December 20, 1800, speaks of Yonge Street between Queen Street and Yorkville as "the road to Yonge Street". The meeting was held to consider the best means of opening the road, enabling farmers to bring their produce to the town market without having to detour around the entire town.

Chief-Justice Elmsley didn't think the work could be done for less than $500.

A proposal was soon accepted to open and make the road passable at the rate of $12 per acre for clearing; and approximately $1.50 per 16½-feet (1 rod) for making a causeway 18-feet wide.

This work was completed in June, 1802, and the road continued to be known for some years as "the road to Yonge Street".

The work for improving the street included cutting tree stumps level with the ground, levelling small hills, filling up valleys, making the surface of the road smooth and free from any obstructions and at least 18-feet wide along the centre of the road, and building a ditch of not less than three-feet to carry off the water.

There were adequate slopes to drain low-lying bushlands extending to the west, but ditches were not constructed for many years afterward. Consequently, the streets of York extended into undrained swamp lands; and much of the area, until 1834 when municipal government was established, was a dangerous bog in wet season.

He rode on horseback up Yonge Street in 1801 to locate farm lots for the party of settlers he was planning to bring into Upper Canada. Up the great road he went, with his wife Sarah and the entourage of some 27 families from Vermont and Connecticut: Timothy Rogers was a miller, merchant and a pious Quaker. He opened a wagon road up Yonge Street and founded the first successful settlement in the townships of King and Whitchurch.

There was a stability of character in the Quaker Settlements that gave strength to the pioneer community of Upper Canada. They gave Yonge Street settlements a measure of discipline and law and order in the frontier society. Yet there was little even they could do to improve the state of the road.

The town of York, by 1805, boasted 119 men, 82 women, 25 children and 55 servants.

From 1803 onwards, Governor Peter Hunter (1799 - 1805) felt that the state of the roads in winter made meetings of the Legislature more feasible; yet it was still a great challenge to reach the capital by land anytime during the year.

One of the great horrors of Yonge Street was the ascent and descent of the Rosedale Ravine where Yonge Street crossed it. The gorge was commonly referred to as the Blue Hill because of the bluish clay at the summit of both sides.

Two slopes were cut into the ravine's lofty banks to accommodate the Yonge Street wagon track which passed up and down the slopes with great difficulty. After autumn rains and spring thaws, it became almost hopeless to travel along this stretch of road. The brook at the top of the hill was known as Castle Frank Creek, the stream which ran through Simcoe's summer home among the pines on the Don River.

Just north of Blue Hill was another place to be avoided—Summer Hill, just south of St. Clair Avenue, with a wide view of the plain below. The grade of this steep hill was partially reduced by pick and shovel, creating a sunken road where it reached the top. The primitive wagon track of Yonge Street ascended the hill and passed through this narrow excavated notch or trench along the trail.

To the north of what is now Yonge and College, a wooden tramway was constructed over a short distance on Yonge Street. This was a blessing for the farmers who travelled along the road after a heavy rainstorm. The tramway was suggested by Rowland Burr who emigrated from Pennsylvania in 1803. He was a born engineer who masterminded the cutting down of the Blue Hill, despite such "minor" problems as subterranean springs and quicksands. At the close of 1803, the town plot of York measured some 420 acres, with 456 people within its boundaries and a property value of nearly $60,000.

A valiant effort was made, in 1807, to improve the road at Blue Hill. A group of enthusiastic citizens gathered to cut down the hill at Frank's Creek, a minor branch of the Don River, and in an effort to help, Lieutenant-Governor Gore (1806 - 1817) sent a messenger to the site with a donation of $50 to help improve the Yonge Street road at that point.

Yonge Street also saw its share of hostilities. It was certainly not uncommon by the turn of the century to settle private quarrels by duelling. January 3, 1800, John White, the first Attorney-General of Upper Canada, was killed in a duel with John Small, the Clerk of the Executive Council.

One day in 1817, eighteen-year-old John Ridout, son of the Surveyor-General Thomas Ridout, demanded a sum of money from Samuel Jarvis Senior, Registrar of the Province. Jarvis was annoyed by Ridout's rude and hostile manner and threw him out of his office. Some time later, Ridout ambushed Jarvis, hit him with a stick, and in the early morning of July 12th, they faced each other in a duel. It was in Elmsley field, northwest of the corner of Yonge and College; it was the last duel fought in York.

Ridout fired prematurely at the count of 'two'. Some say the bullet was fired into the air, and others said it hit Jarvis' neck cloth. Ridout's pistol was taken from him for a second, and at the count of 'three' Jarvis fired, killing his unarmed opponent.

Jarvis was charged with manslaughter but was acquitted.

Eleven years later, the seconds of the duel, H.J. Boulton and James Small, were brought to trial for their part in the duel as accessories, but they too were acquitted.

In 1807, plans for turnpiking Yonge Street began. It was suggested that all stumps and boulders be removed from the centre of the road and that the edges be ploughed to provide drainage by use of ditches and road-crowning. By 1816, some of the stumps and large roots had been removed, but wagon travel was still extremely slow; there were too many mud holes, and bridges were often washed out by floods.

Before any kind of pavement was attempted on Yonge Street, the sidewalks in some parts were made clean and comfortable by a thick coating of tan-bark. Cattle strayed into the street although a board fence 5-feet high hid the back lots from Yonge Street and kept out stray dogs and wild pigs.

Gravel was finally laid on the street in 1828. Cedar-block paving of the 1870s was the last road surface before the brick, concrete and asphalt surfaces we know today.

North Into the Wilderness   5

DURING SIMCOE'S REGIME, Yonge Street was the only road leading north into the untamed wilderness. By 1797, it was the major link along which many of the provisions came to the north from the farms in the south.

Simcoe felt the location of a port in the upper lakes region at Matchedash Bay was extremely important, and also realized the potential of this new route between Huron and Montreal over that of the less appealing Ottawa River with its treacherous rapids.

"Lake Simcoe is capable of admitting any vessel, and its banks afford birch of sufficient size for the largest canoes. . . the agricultural part of this country will materially assist the commercial, by the transport during the continuance of the winter season of the goods in sleighs over these portages and Lake . . . in particular in the conveyance of heavy articles and provisions."[41]

In the spring of 1794, Simcoe asked Alexander Aitkin to journey north to Matchedash Bay to explore a 14-mile portage route between the narrows on Lake Simcoe and Matchedash Bay, and to survey a site at Penetanguishene for a further naval base. He was, however, diverted from that task for a short time. A loyalist from New Brunswick named John Wilson had arrived in Niagara in October, 1793, with a party of 43 people who were destitute and starving to death. They were given permission to come to York, and in the spring of 1794, they settled on Yonge Street. Aitkin was instructed to open Yonge Street "as far back as may be necessary for the settlement of Mr. Wilson and his associates."[42]

In the autumn of 1794, Aitkin resumed his duties and crossed over Lake Simcoe to Matchedash Bay. Simcoe wanted to establish a settlement at the end of Lake Simcoe and another at Matchedash Bay.

The intervening land was to be used for portage routes and farmland, furthering the development of Yonge Street and his grand dream.

During his early expedition to Lake Simcoe and Matchedash Bay in 1793, Simcoe had followed the Severn River to its mouth and reached the open waters of Matchedash Bay. Between Lake Simcoe and Georgian Bay was the country of the "Torontogueronons", or "the people who live at Toronto". The shortest route between these two bodies of water, one which shortened the entire water route by some 50 miles, was an 18-mile overland trail known as the Matchedash Portage, Iroquois Trail or Coldwater Trail. This trail was clearly marked out and labelled as Yonge Street on a map of 1800. *Smith's Gazetteer* of 1799 speaks of this portage trail from Lake Simcoe to Matchedash Bay by way of Coldwater and calls it a "continuation of Yonge Street."[43] The entire route from York to Michilimackinac was also considered to be Yonge Street, at least in the eyes of the North West Company.

This Coldwater Trail was also included in the plans for a communication between Lake Ontario and Lake Huron as originally conceived by Frobisher, de Rocheblave and Collins. With his pioneer verve and enthusiasm, Simcoe was quick to give the name Yonge Street to the northern link as well as to that section between York and Holland Landing.

The Coldwater Trail ran from the narrows between Lake Simcoe and Lake Couchiching in a northwesterly direction, along the north side of Bass Lake to Coldwater River in Tay Township, and Matchedash Bay and Sturgeon Bay. It was the main route to Penetanguishene and the shortest way to Lake Huron.

Alexander Aitkin, who made the first detailed map of the region, wasn't too impressed with the possibility of constructing a road along the Coldwater Trail. On his map he made the following notation next to the dotted line marked as an "Indian Road": "This country will not admit of a good summer road but may (be made) to answer in winter for sleighs."[44]

This original trail was first cleared out as a road for vehicles in 1830, when Sir John Colborne, Governor of Upper Canada (1828 - 1836), brought together the Ojibway Indian tribes of the area to create an Indian reserve.

Because it was developed so much later, the name Yonge Street has never been attached to the route which is now known as the Coldwater Road or Highway no. 12. The latter follows the course of the original trail between Orillia and Coldwater.

Aitkin found Penetanguishene to be ideal for a town and harbour, and both he and Simcoe had high hopes of this route being better and more prosperous than the round-about journey they made during their expedition in 1793.

Although Aitkin realized that the trail could be made into a good winter road, he also discovered that four carrying places or portages along the trail could be avoided by using several water channels along the same route they used in the '73 expedition.

Simcoe wrote to Dorchester indicating he wanted to purchase a small piece of land including Penetanguishene and the harbour at Sturgeon Bay. On May 19, 1795, the Penetanguishene Purchase was agreed upon and was officially ratified at York in May, 1798.

Smith's Gazetteer of 1799 extolled the great advantage of this continuation of Yonge Street "in the future of transporting merchandise from Oswego to York, and from thence across Yonge Street and down the waters of lake Simcoe into lake Huron, in preference to sending it by Lake Erie."[45]

A continuation of Yonge Street was surveyed and opened some time later by the military unit of Simcoe, from Kempenfelt Bay on Lake Simcoe (east of Barrie) to Penetanguishene.

Kempenfelt Bay was named after Admiral Kempenfelt whose ship, the Royal George, was sunk at Spithead in 1782 while undergoing repairs.

The North West Company   6

I T WAS SIMCOE'S AMBITION to induce traders to follow his route from York on Lake Ontario to Matchedash Bay on Georgian Bay. He regarded Yonge Street as the potential channel by which all the wealth of the west would funnel through York, which at that time had no other signs of prosperity.

As much as $72 per ton could be saved by transporting goods up Yonge Street to the northwest posts rather than by way of the Ottawa River, a fact which made the route attractive to traders.

The wilderness headquarters for the North West Company was on Lake Superior at Kaministikwia — a booming frontier town of 3,000 people, situated near the present site of Thunder Bay. The financial headquarters of the company was in Montreal, then a metropolis of fur-trade moguls who later came to occupy seats in the Legislature and Councils of Canada and Britain.

The company's supplies came from Oswego in New York State, were lifted over the peninsula and travelled up the Don River to York Mills. There, the freight was loaded onto wagons for the long and rough trip up Yonge Street to the Holland River, Lake Simcoe and finally to Lake Huron.

Between 1799 and the War of 1812, it was reported that the North West Company donated thousands of pounds towards improving the great Canadian road. "We hear that the N.W. Company has given twelve thousand pounds towards making Yonge Street a good road, and the N.W. commerce will be communicated through this place."[46]

Before and during the War of 1812, the North West Company showed a strong interest in the Yonge Street route, but because of financial difficulties and the company's take-over and amalgamation by the Hudson's Bay Company in 1821, this interest was short-lived.

The fur trade did not develop as was hoped. The St. Lawrence River system and the Yonge Street route were no longer important routes for the company, which used a Hudson's Bay route. Toronto's future expansion was not to be dependent on the business of fur trading after all.

If a large trade had developed, a wharf would probably have been built at the foot of Yonge Street and the condition of the road between Yorkville and Queen Street would have improved much earlier. As it was, Yonge Street did not extend south of Queen until 1818; and even as late as 1847 a team of oxen could be seen stationed just north of Queen Street, ready to haul wagons out of one of the many mud holes that decorated the thoroughfare.

In the heyday of the fur business, there were many Montreal traders who still preferred using the Detroit and Ottawa routes, even though the former was in the hands of the Americans.

The traders were skeptical about following a route through an independent Upper Canada where traders might be restrained by decisions of a new government and its legal system.

At Detroit they had their own ships which could be sent directly to Michilimackinac and later on to the post at St. Joseph Island in the North Channel of Lake Huron just before entering Lake Superior. A garrison was set up there to protect the business which radiated from all directions.

The powerful Niagara-Detroit merchants had no intention of losing one dollar's business to the Montreal merchants and kept a tight hold on the fur trade — a task made easy because of close connections with the merchants in Montreal.

With the development of the Yonge Street route north to Michilimackinac and St. Joseph Island, a regular mid-winter express or postal service was established, passing along the northern route to the fort at St. Joseph Island.

Many of the letters to and from the island contained some very interesting information concerning Yonge Street and the intentions of the North West Company.

Writing to his brother in Queenston on August 11th, 1811, John Askin (appointed Indian interpreter at St. Joseph) wrote in one letter: ". . . should the N.W. Gentlemen establish the road as is proposed from York to Matchedash, it will be the making of the country."[47]

D'Arcy Boulton, who settled in York in 1803, published his

account of Upper Canada in London in 1805: "This great communication (Yonge Street) . . . is calculated to attract the attention of the North West Company. It is considerably shorter than the route by the Straights of Niagara and Detroit."[48]

Samuel Street Wilmot, Deputy Surveyor, was sent to explore the territory between Kempenfelt Bay on Lake Simcoe and Penetanguishene on Georgian Bay, in March of 1808, with the purpose of building a road for the use of the North West Company. One of the company's agents, Angus Shaw, accompanied Wilmot on a journey to the area two years later to examine the prospects for a road. At that time Wilmot was to "lay off a road from Kempenfelt Bay on Lake Simcoe to Lake Huron (Georgian Bay) into lots, and a village at each extremity of the road",[49] a task he hoped to finish by Christmas 1810.

Wilmot began his survey in the summer of 1811, however, on the north side of Kempenfelt Bay near the place at the head of the Bay where in 1808 his examination of the line took place. At this point he was to choose the best place for a townsite and harbour, both at Kempenfelt and Penetanguishene, and lay-off lots for settlement along the road. His survey line for a 30-mile road was completed in October of that year.

In the late fall of 1810, Archibald McLeod travelled to Fort William to attend a general meeting of the North West Company. The written summary which was later drawn up revealed that United States' Customs officials had been interfering with the business of the company since 1796 ; and having had their boats and property seized, the North West Company decided to take all their trade by way of York and up Yonge Street. In return, they asked for a grant of 2,000 acres of land at Penetanguishene and Kempenfelt Bay and 200 acres at Holland Landing. In the winter of 1812, the required grants of land were made, but deeds were not issued, and the land between Kempenfelt and Penetanguishene was not actually purchased from the Indians until 1815.

While their request was being considered by the British Government, war was declared in June of 1812 and the government was no longer in a position to bargain with the North West Company.

Movement of supplies to the northwest posts in summer stopped as the route was abandoned for another trail.

Instead of proceeding overland from Kempenfelt Bay to Penetanguishene, Samuel Wilmot and Angus Shaw were determined to use

16 Henry Burt Williams' omnibus.

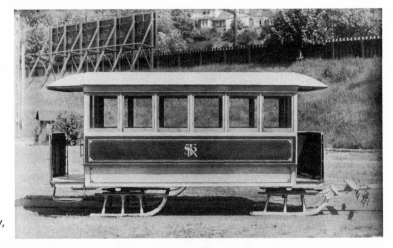

17 The Toronto Street Railway, sleigh.

18 Toronto's first two-horse open car.

another route to Penetanguishene — the Willow Creek Portage to the Nottawasaga River, and a second portage to the head of the harbour at Penetanguishene. At the west end of Kempenfelt Bay near the present site of Barrie, a 9-mile portage led northwest to Willow Creek which is a tributary of the Nottawasaga River. Willow trees had to be cut away from the water's edge to make it navigable for military boats.

During the War of 1812 and for several years afterwards, supplies en route to British posts were transported up the Yonge Street route and then shipped through Lake Simcoe to the head of Kempenfelt Bay. From there the Nine-Mile Portage Trail lead to Willow Creek which in turn lead to the Nottawasaga River and eventually to Georgian Bay. This shortened the overland route north to Lake Simcoe to the west by 16 miles and was used by the military during the War of 1812.

A Government Reserve was established at Kempenfelt. The actual cutting-out and construction of the road was proposed in 1813, after the survey had been completed in the latter part of 1811. *Smith's Gazetteer* indicated that a tract of land had been purchased from the Indians and that a road would soon be opening between the two bodies of water in question, which would enable the North West Company to transport their good from York to Lake Huron by avoiding the round-about route of Lake Erie and the American frontier.

Delay was inevitable. Competition with the Hudson's Bay Company and financial problems forced the North West Company to economize and alter their aims. During the war years the North West Company had to put a damper on their plans to use the York - Penetanguishene line of communication.

Dr. William "Tiger" Dunlop, better known as the "Warden of the Woods" for the Canada Company, cut out the road from Kempenfelt to Penetanguishene with a military party, an engineer and a company of French Canadian axemen, and began the first stage of construction.

In the autumn of 1814 it was decided to establish a dockyard at Penetanguishene making it necessary for a road to be cut to that point — a distance of about 30 miles. Dunlop volunteered to supervise the work and travelled north on Yonge Street to the site. He had little idea of what was in store for him.

When he arrived at Lake Simcoe he found that the lake

was not completely frozen, but two days later he skated across it, and thought it suitable for passage. As his men were about to begin the trek over the ice there was a thunderous crash — the ice had shattered all over the lake. Dunlop quickly organized a rope-line and they dragged their hand-sleighs, each one packed with provisions and tools, across the precarious surface of the lake. One man plunged through the ice and was dragged out again by his comrades. It took 6 hours for Dunlop and his men to reach the other side of the lake.

Dunlop and his men then trudged onward through between 3-feet of snow. Some wore snowshoes and marched Indian-style.

After erecting shanties the men began the actual job of road building. They had to do all the packing and unpacking and carry supplies, since the horses and oxen were rendered immobile by the deep snow. Cold, tired and hungry men hauled logs from swamps through thick mounds of snow, using drag ropes and standing for hours up to their waists in ice-cold water.

"I would undertake tomorrow to cut a better road than we could possibly do, for forty pounds a mile (for a distance of 30 miles), and make money by it; give me timely warning and a proper season of the year; whereas I am convinced that 2,500 to 3,000 pounds did not pay for the one we cut," [50] Dunlop was reported as saying.

Just as the road was nearing completion word was received that the war had ended, and all were ordered home.

For several years after the war Lake Simcoe remained the only connecting link from York to Penetanguishene. Cattle were ferried across Cook Bay in a scow, from Roches Point to De Grassi Point. From there they were driven north along a winding Indian trail through the township of Innisfil to the head of Kempenfelt Bay, and then to Penetanguishene by way of the road finally opened by Dunlop in 1814-15. Three years later, lots of 200 acres were laid out along the new road in the same manner as those on Yonge Street.

By 1825, Yonge Street had been extended in a very rough fashion, north from Holland Landing to the Coulson Settlement in the north section of West Gwillimbury Township. North from there through the township of Innisfil to the other section of road already constructed at the head of Kempenfelt Bay by Dunlop was an unbroken wilderness.

Settlers from Penetanguishene raised a sum of money by subscription to join the two sections of road together — the part ending at the Coulson Settlement and that part from Kempenfelt to Penetanguishene. John and George Warnica of Innisfil earned $5 per mile and opened the road from Kempenfelt Bay south to the site of Churchill, a distance of 11 miles. They also opened the remaining section from there south to West Gwillimbury. By the fall of 1825 the work had been completed. The new road was called Main Street, or "Main Road", connecting the Coulson Settlement with Kempenfelt Bay and the Penetanguishene Road.

The Yonge Street extension from Holland Landing to Kempenfelt Bay was still a zigzag road fit for horseback riding and not too much else.

Sir John Franklin, explorer, travelled up Yonge Street in 1825, en route to the Arctic in search of a northwest passage from the Atlantic Ocean to the Pacific Ocean. He stopped at Newmarket, crossed Lake Simcoe by canoe and continued to Penetanguishene via the new road.

The route from York to Penetanguishene was made in two weeks. From there to the northwest trading posts the route skirted the shores of Lake Huron and Lake Superior.

The government, by 1830, opened the portage route between . the Indian station at Orillia and Coldwater, along the Coldwater River which led to Matchedash Bay; and extended the route 5 miles further into Sturgeon Bay.

The Penetanguishene Road or the Yonge Street extension, as it was often called, 30 miles long and 66-feet wide, was cleared out and made suitable for general travel in 1847.

PRESIDENT MADISON OF THE UNITED STATES declared war on Great Britain on June 18, 1812. To the people of Canada this meant the immediate danger of an invasion.

A group of young Congressmen from the south called the "War Hawks" welcomed with open arms a chance to retaliate against Britain by attacking her scattered and defenceless colonies in North America. They wanted the American flag to wave in the land of the British Colonies and thus strengthen their control over North America.

Under the terms of "Jay's Treaty" in 1794, the British had agreed to abandon their military outpost at Michilimackinac and had moved their forces to St. Joseph Island two years later.

But in 1812 an expedition from St. Joseph Island, commanded by Captain Charles Roberts, set out to capture American-held Michilimackinac. The mission was successful and secured the northwest for the British during the war.

The small British garrison stationed there sent word to Kingston asking for reinforcements when it was discovered that the Americans had every intention of recapturing Michilimackinac — a strategic military location in the Upper lakes region. Ten officers, 200 men, 20 artillery-men, a lieutenant and 20 men of the Royal Navy left Kingston in February of 1814 under the command of Lieutenant-Colonel Robert McDowall. Marching through the wilderness to Toronto, they proceeded north up Yonge Street to Holland Landing. They crossed Lake Simcoe on ice and on the banks of the Nottawasaga River they built 29 light flat-bottomed boats while waiting for the ice on the river to break up. They advanced again on April 22, 1814.

After a gruelling 300-mile journey in open boats, amidst blocks of floating ice and buffeted by fierce storms, they reached Michilimackinac on May 18, 1814, and held the fort against an American attack on July 28th.

At the end of the war Michilimackinac was returned to the Americans and in 1815 a new British military post was established on Drummond Island (southeast of St. Joseph Island). In 1828, Drummond Island was given to the Americans and the British forces withdrew to Penetanguishene.

Some improvement was made to Yonge Street before the war, but the dirt track was a veritable slough in heavy rain and was rivetted with ruts in winter. During the war heavy traffic along the road made it necessary for continuous repairs. In some cases the troops had a hard time trying to move overland along the road and often left their baggage stuck in the mud.

In 1814, more money was voted upon for use on highways, and many improvements were made. A traveller in 1816 thought Yonge Street was one of the best roads he had seen; this gentleman was perhaps not a seasoned traveller.

After York's surrender the Americans sent search parties up Yonge Street to confiscate supplies. Canadian troops were literally forced into using the Yonge Street route to Lake Huron. They needed far more supplies than Upper Canada could produce and since the Americans on Lake Erie made the western route to the Upper Lakes an unsafe venture, Yonge Street was chosen as the alternative.

Travel By Stage Coach 8

THE USUAL MODE OF TRAVEL in the 1820s was the horse-drawn wagon. But those who travelled the great Canadian road in the early years preferred to go by horseback rather than a wagon, as the latter was slow and uncomfortable. The condition of Yonge Street had improved but there were still many mud holes which remained a bog all year round; blowing clouds of dust and sand were also common in dry weather; bridges were often destroyed by floods; and the logs of the corduroy section of the road made wagon travel a nightmare.

In the 1830s several rudimentary sewers were constructed and drained the worst areas of the town; but major improvements would require building a bridge over the Don River and its tributaries. These could not be considered, since a budget of only 50 pounds was all that was available for the work.

But as more and more people settled along the route, there came a need for improved transportation. The lumber trade expanded and opened up the northern area of the Yonge Street townships, and many sawmills were built in the predominantly hardwood forests. The village of Holland Landing came into existence as more people settled in the township of West Gwillimbury.

The *Upper Canada Gazette* and *Weekly Register* of August, 1825, advertised that Lewis Bapp had begun to operate a light covered wagon service between York and Holland Landing twice a week.

In 1828, the Yonge Street Stage was launched; five years later it offered a daily service. The same year George Playter began to run a stage coach line between York and Holland Landing, providing the weather was suitable for travel. One year later, George Playter and Sons' first stage coach line was in full swing, making regular stops at wayside inns and taverns along the route.

The booking office for Playter's line was in a livery stable in downtown York. The Red Lion Inn was the only tavern in the area of Bloor and Yonge at that time; and beyond that the stage coach driver faced driving his vehicle through mud and over the hills and hollows of the Davenport Ridge, the Blue Hill, Gallows Hill, Hogg's Hollow, Thorn's Hill, Richmond Hill and the Oak Hills or Ridges. Thorn's Hill was named after Benjamin Thorne who built a sawmill, the largest tannery in Canada, a flour mill, a brick plant and a general store. Oak Ridges was a strip of elevated and irregular ground.

An announcement in the *Colonial Advocate*, September, 1829, gave schedules and prices: "The (Newmarket) Mail Stage will start from Joseph Bloor's Hotel . . . on Mondays and Thursdays at 12 o'clock noon and arrive at 9 o'clock the same evening in Newmarket; and will leave Mr. Barber's Tavern, Newmarket, for York on Wednesdays and Saturdays, at 6 in the morning, and arrive in York at 2 p.m. on the same days. Prices for passengers . . . six shillings and three pence currency, and in proportion for shorter distances. . .Passengers . . . may be . . . conveyed to Holland Landing, or in other directions if required."[51]

William Weller of Cobourg became the most prominent stage coach proprietor of Upper Canada. A former Mayor of Cobourg for three years, he owned stage lines to Kingston, Dundas and Niagara.

In the summer of 1830, Weller operated a stage coach service twice a week between York, Cobourg and the Carrying Place which was near Trenton at the Bay of Quinte. Here, a steamboat met the stage to and from Kingston.

Two years later, he bought George Playter's line. The coaches were bright yellow and each was drawn by four imported Irish stock mares with the King's coat-of-arms inscribed on the side of each coach. The clatter of horses' hoofs along the rutted country lane of Yonge Street to Holland Landing and the swirls of dust billowing in the wake of the coach announced its arrival at designated inns and taverns along the way.

Weller's line was also referred to as William Weller's Royal Mail Line. The baggage was loaded on top of the roof and in the large wooden compartment behind the passengers' compartment. The driver sat on top of a high wooden platform similar to the one in the back of the coach, which also contained the Royal Mail bags for each postal community along the route. In order to deliver the mail on time as agreed upon with the government and get the travellers to their destination to make other connections, Weller was obliged to drive his coaches quickly over the bumpy road.

It must certainly have been a sad sight, yet comical in a way, to see the passengers prying the coach out of the slithering slime and mire with the aid of fence rails or logs, especially during a rainstorm.

Charles Poulett Thompson of Summer Hill also operated an early stage line on Yonge Street in the 1830s. Thompson was a well-known stage coach driver on the Toronto-Newmarket route.

"A stage leaves York (the coach office was at the corner of Front and Market or Wellington Streets, just east of Yonge) every day at 12 o'clock and arrives at Phelps' Inn, Holland Landing, at 7 o'clock the same evening."[52]

From the forests of Sunnidale Township where Thompson had a house, he made a trip down Yonge Street by stage in 1834 on one of his first business trips to York. He started out on foot from his home, and reached Yonge where he took the stage. "The day's journey by way of Yonge Street was easily accomplished by stage — an old fashioned conveyance — swung on leather straps and subject to tremendous jerks and loose stones on the rough road. A fellow passenger . . . told me how an old man . . . had been jolted so violently against the roof, as to leave marks of his blood there . . .My friend advised me to keep on my hat."[53]

In 1831, a steamboat called The Colborne was built. Two years later, Thompson bought it and put it into service north of Holland Landing to run in conjunction with his Yonge Street Stage line.

There was another steamboat, called The Beaver, built in 1844, which was also part of the stage line. It was jointly owned by Thompson and a Captain Laughton. This partnership lasted for six years until a misunderstanding between the two men caused them to go their separate ways. They were to become bitter rivals.

Laughton established a rival stage line on Yonge Street about 1850, and Thompson, meanwhile, built a steamboat called The Morning and operated it against Laughton's boat. Thompson's stage line, the Northern Mail and Stage Coach, left Toronto from the Simcoe stage office on Church Street for Holland Landing and connected with the steamboat, The Morning. Laughton's stage left Toronto from the Western Hotel, at Wellington Street just east of Yonge Street, for Holland Landing and connected with the steamboat The

19 Robert Simpson   *20   Timothy Eaton*

21 The Henry Burt Williams omnibus at the Red Lion Hotel, 1850.

Beaver. The 35-mile journey to Holland Landing was completed in about six or seven hours.

Laughton extended his stage service north of Lake Simcoe with the addition of another steamboat, The Gore, on Lake Huron.

His stage line soon became known as The People's Line of Stages, and travelled through York Mills, Thornhill, Richmond Hill, Whitchurch Village, Newmarket, Holland Landing and arrived at Bradford. From there, passengers could board The Beaver for the distant ports of Barrie, Orillia, Penetanguishene, Owen Sound, Manitoulin, Wallace Mine, St. Joseph, Bruce Mine and Sault Ste. Marie. The two men's rivalry continued until the coming of the Northern Railway.

Another prominent figure of stage coach travel in 1837 was Thomas McCausland who operated a mail stage for travellers between Holland Landing and Barrie. He first carried the mail to Barrie on horseback then added another route from Barrie to Bradford to connect with the Toronto mail run by way of the Yonge Street stage line, thereby establishing a direct mail service between Toronto and Barrie.

The British post office was reluctant to use postal routes which would lose money and a regular postal service was slow to be established. Meanwhile letters were delivered by servants and couriers throughout the villages.

With the advent of the stage coach lines, mail was dispatched from Toronto to Holland Landing three times a week. On the Wednesday trip, the same stage carried mail to the half dozen offices in the northern wilderness. Where stage travel was impossible in the north, the mail was carried on foot or on horseback.

The stage coach carried wagon loads of farm produce and assorted merchandise; two stage coaches made daily trips north to make connections with The Beaver and The Morning on Lake Simcoe. Another coach was operated by Tom and Bill Cook of Yorkshire House at Langstaff; it ran between Toronto and Richmond Hill, picking up passengers and mail bags. Cost was about 75 cents for the three-hour journey.

There was no regular line of stage coach service between Barrie and Penetanguishene until 1847. "Comfortable coaches are in attendance at Barrie, every Monday and Friday, on the arrival of the steamboat Beaver, from Holland Landing for the immediate conveyance of passengers to Penetanguishene."[54] The fare from Barrie to Penetanguishene was 7 shillings and 6 pence.

In the same year, a Mr. Shuttleworth began to operate a

65

second kind of stage coach service on Yonge Street by using omnibuses only as far north as Richmond Hill. Henry Burt Williams, a Toronto cabinet maker, is credited, however, with being the first to originate and operate such a bus which was smaller than the stage coach with little or no room for luggage.

The first omnibus was a 6-passenger vehicle; the windows could be closed with leather curtains, and the fare was the old English sixpence. In 1849, Williams operated a line of 4 buses (omnibuses) from the St. Lawrence Market, and from King and Yonge, to the Red Lion Inn at the present site of Yorkville Avenue. Buses ran every ten minutes from either end and became an instant success. In 1850, Williams built four larger, 10-passenger buses which continued to operate for twelve years until he sold out to the Toronto Street Railway Company.

When Yonge Street was at its worst, both driver and passengers had to resort to creative thinking in order to get the stage coach up a steep incline. Heavy ropes were often tied from the coach to a tree on a nearby hilltop; driver and passengers combined their strength in an effort to help the horses and coach up the slope. It was common for passengers to get out of the coach to help lift the front wheels out of a pitch-hole.

The stage coach was equipped with shovels and axes to help the driver and the passengers dig their way out of a swamp or remove fallen trees from the road.

The stage coach drivers also had to beware of the laws of the road. A statute was passed in 1812 requiring all vehicles to keep to the right of the road. There was also a police regulation making it necessary to have at least two bells attached to a harness to warn of oncoming traffic. In 1817, a regulation made it illegal to drive at an unreasonable speed. This was also when the first parking regulation was introduced, making it unlawful to leave wagons on the street for more than twenty four hours.

The coming of the stage to each village along the route was a big event. The driver would sound his horn and the residents of the village would crowd around the vehicle, watching the changing of the horses and the arrival of passengers and mail.

During this necessary delay while the mail was being sorted, the stage driver found time to refresh his dry palate in the bar of the inn at which he stopped.

Some drivers worked out deals with certain innkeepers; the

drivers agreeing to bring business to the taverns while the innkeepers offered the drivers free drinks in return. Drinking drivers have apparently been a problem since the earliest days of Yonge Street.

Stage coaches were surprisingly streamlined. The sides were open but protected by leather curtains which could be lowered in case of rain. At the rear of the coach was a baggage rack for trunks, protected by a large leather cloth. Lighter luggage was stored on the roof which was surrounded by a light iron railing. The coach itself was suspended on sturdy leather straps stretched along the framework of the carriage. There was a door at each side, with a sliding window which could be lowered or raised.

Wooden boxes fastened to iron runners were pulled by horses and oxen to transport winter freight over the road.

By 1850, the Concord stage coach, originally built by Abott and Downing of Concord, New Hampshire, was in virtually exclusive use on Yonge Street. As there were several coach builders in Toronto at the time, the Concord coaches were probably built here.

The Concord was built for heavy service; the carriage was suspended by two braces of sole oxhide, eight layers thick, to reduce the bumping and jolting. The hard seats of the early coaches were replaced by more comfortable seats and no one could complain of this stage being just another rickety box on wheels or runners.

The stage coaches were longer and lower than the previous models. Some (1841 model) had a movable seat between the doors which could hold two people. One had four doors and three fixed seats — this was used mostly as a winter coach or sleigh. The usual load was eight or nine passengers who sat inside the carriage with one or two on top, either beside the driver or over the luggage compartment. Depending upon the day, destination and where one lived, you could transfer from one line to the other.

The omnibus was used for local traffic. It had more room inside with lengthwise benches and a single door at the rear. Mail was carried by the omnibus as far as Richmond Hill until 1896. It was unique in that it was one of the few surviving lines. Most of the important stage routes had been replaced by the railway in the early 1850s. Still by 1880, John Thompson's omnibus made daily return trips from Richmond Hill to Toronto. Returning from Toronto, it would stop at Thornhill (4 miles from Richmond Hill) and a change would be made to a smaller vehicle. Along the route passengers passed such notable inns as Palmer's at Richmond Hill, Lemon's at Thornhill, the Golden Lion at Lansing and the Bay Horse at the city limits.

Passengers riding on top of the stage had to hang on to their hats as the vehicle approached the northern hills and rutted roads; those inside had to cease conversation because of the noise made by the horses' hoofs and iron wheels clattering over cobblestones for part of the journey.

Rye and Rebellion 9

THERE WERE MORE TAVERNS on Yonge Street than on any other road in York.

"Between the head of Kempenfelt Bay at Barrie and Yonge Street Wharf in Toronto there were 68 licensed houses — one for each mile of the road and three to spare, besides eight or ten unlicensed places."[55] By 1850, in the city itself there were 152 taverns and 206 beer shops for a population of 30,000.

The wayside tavern and town inn were the centres of social life. A typical hotel or inn would have a kitchen, barroom and one bedroom with four or five hard-planked beds. It was a log house with pine furniture and a log trough outside for washing. Talking, smoking, drinking, swearing, spitting and scratching mosquito bites were the common activities of the day.

The rural or country inns were built in the 1830s and 1840s to stimulate trade and accommodate new settlers who wanted farmland for themselves. Despite the poor condition of the road and the lack of transportation facilities, the inns were always filled to capacity. Those unable to find a bed slept in the hayloft. Food was cooked in a fireplace and a water pump was provided outside.

One of the earliest and perhaps best respected inns was the Red Lion Inn, built by Daniel Tiers on the east side of Yonge Street just north of Bloor Street with a frontage of about 100-feet. All the stage coach lines that passed up and down the great Canadian road stopped at the Red Lion where customers "will be served with victualating in good order on the shortest notice, and at a cheap rate. He (Tiers) will furnish the best strong beer at 8d. New York currency per gallon if drank in his house, and 2s. 6d.

69

New York currency taken out . . . He will immediately have entertainment for man and horse."[56] The Inn was demolished in 1890.

Thomas Hill ran a tavern on the southwest corner of Sheppard Avenue and Yonge Street in 1802; this was purchased in 1824 by Thomas Sheppard, who built the Golden Lion Hotel, with verandahs and a mud-brick kitchen. Over the main doorway was the famous life-size carving of a lion made by Paul Sheppard from a stump of pine.

George Harrison built one of the best-known inns on Yonge Street in 1841, called the Half-Way House, where horses were changed on the York-Holland Landing stage coach route. It was on an acre of land at the top of the hill on the east side of the street, just north of the present line of the Macdonald-Cartier Freeway.

In 1847, John Morley built a tavern on the northwest corner of Steeles Avenue and Yonge Street; it eventually became known as Steeles Hotel and The Green Bush Inn. John Steele was the proprietor in 1877 (his father, Thomas, was the previous owner).

John Montgomery, in the early 1830s, built a two-storey tavern on the west side of Yonge Street near Montgomery Avenue, and it became known as Montgomery's Tavern or the Sickle and Sheath. It was a tavern that soon took its place in history as the focal point for the Rebellion of 1837.

November 25, 1837, William Lyon Mackenzie published a 'Declaration of Independence' in his own newspaper, *The Colonial Advocate*, calling for a rebellion — an armed revolt against the government of the day.

Mackenzie was a wiry and quick-tempered Scotsman, the brave, energetic leader of the radical wing of the Reformers in the Legislative Assembly. In 1834, the year in which York became Toronto, he became its first mayor. In his youth he had been a bookseller, druggist, editor and publisher of *The Colonial Advocate* in 1824 at the age of 29, and a Member of Parliament.

He was inclined to distrust anyone in authority; and in his first issue of *The Colonial Advocate* he accused reigning Lieutenant-Governor Maitland (1818-1828) of being to blame for the lack of progress in the province. Mackenzie proposed new programs for reform but these were dismissed by the government. But Mackenzie had many political friends and public supporters who agreed for the most part with his ideas for reform. And in 1837 he decided to try and achieve his reforms through a surprise attack on the city — an undertaking which ended in disaster.

Mackenzie's rendezvous point was Montgomery's Tavern, 4 miles north of the city, from where he and his rebels would set out to attack the city of Toronto on the night of December 7, 1837, under the command of Colonel Anthony Van Egmond who had been a French officer under Napoleon. He expected at least 5,000 men to join him at Montgomery's Tavern, which he used as his headquarters, but only a few hundred rebel supporters showed up for the march.

Mackenzie and his men planned to take the Governor into custody and hang him on his own flagpole, "'place the garrison in the hands of the liberals, declare the Province free and call a convention together to frame a new constitution."[57]

Lieutenant-Governor Sir Francis Bond Head, not believing that such a rebellion would take place, ordered most of his troops to Lower Canada, leaving one soldier, 6,000 unpacked muskets and three cannons behind.

But Dr. John Rolph, who had been chosen the new president of Mackenzie's Republic, decided to change the day of attack to December 4th, instead of December 7th, the original date set for the rebellion.

During that bitter cold afternoon, small groups of men carrying pitchforks, rifles and clubs began their trek along Yonge Street towards Montgomery's Tavern. On the way they captured all known Tories and made them their prisoners.

The first of the cold, weary and hungry rebels arrived at the tavern at about 8 o'clock on the evening of December 4th, only to find that no food had been prepared for them. A short time later, however, a meagre dinner was rummaged from the neighbourhood; and two of their leaders, Samuel Lount and Captain Anthony Anderson arrived.

Part of the rebels' plan was to post a group of guards at various intervals along Yonge Street on either side of the tavern to stop all travellers and take them prisoner, until they had enough men to march into the city and overrun the government.

Early that night Colonel Robert Moodie, a veteran of the Napoleonic wars, rode up to the tavern with two other men and was confronted by some 300 armed men. Samuel Lount, who stood guard, refused to let them pass and told them they were now prisoners, but Moodie was determined to go through the barricade and proceed to Toronto; but Lount ordered his men to fire. Three shots rang out in the night. One hit Moodie and killed him on

22 *The John Thompson Stage at Richmond Hill, 1896.*

23 *Yonge and Adelaide Streets, looking north, Pretoria Day, June 5, 1901.*

the spot. His last word was "Charge!" as if he were in the midst of a battle of epic proportions. The rebels tried to detain the rest of Moodie's party but two of his men escaped to the Bloor Street tollgate where they met Mackenzie himself; again they escaped into the city.

Later that night Alderman John Powell and a man named Archibald McDonald rode up Yonge Street to gather as much information as they could regarding the possibility of an armed attack, for they also knew that Governor Bond Head, who refused to barricade the road, was fast asleep and not in the least bit worried. When Powell and McDonald reached Gallows Hill they were surprised by four horsemen who suddenly appeared from the gloomy shadows of the night. They were Mackenzie, Anderson and two others. Powell and McDonald were taken prisoner and forced to march north on Yonge. Powell knew that the city of Toronto was unprepared for an attack; he also knew that his friend McDonald was unarmed. Powell drew a pistol from under his coat, fired at Anderson, who fell to the ground without so much as uttering one word, and in the confusion that followed, galloped down the road to safety. McDonald, however, was recaptured at the Bloor Street tollgate and taken prisoner.

The first news that armed men were about to march down Yonge Street was given to city officials by a young Loyalist, Richard Frizzell.

"Tell them the rebels are coming down Yonge Street," said Frizzell to the police officer stationed at the city hall door, "and that there is a person at the door who can give them information which . . . they should possess."[58]

John Cameron, a barrister's apprentice, rang the bell of Upper Canada College that night; and by midnight the rebels at Montgomery's Tavern received word that the entire city had been alerted to the proposed attack.

Nevertheless, they were determined to carry on with their plans and to march down Yonge Street into the city.

Tuesday morning, December 5th, the City of Toronto was completely paralysed. All business came to a dead halt.

The rebel army at Montgomery's Tavern numbered about 800. Some were confused, some had no guns and some went back home.

They marched down Yonge Street that afternoon and stopped after only a mile at the upper edge of Gallows Hill to re-form

73

their ranks. Their hats were pulled down to ear level and their heavy wooden-soled shoes made walking difficult. The front line of Mackenzie's rebels consisted of several dozen riflemen; the rest of them were armed with pikes, pitchforks and cudgels.

Before the hour of two, the time set for the last stage of the march on Toronto, Samuel Lount's men, still on the slopes of Gallows Hill, caught sight of a small party of men riding towards them carrying a flag of truce, sent from the city by the government. Mackenzie and his men promised to march no further south than the Red Lion Inn and the Bloor Street tollgate; but the government withdrew its offer of truce.

"In the gathering darkness of the late December afternoon (about 6:10 p.m. December 9th), the rebel army trudged on down Yonge Street (from the Bloor Street tollgate), with a few dozen riflemen at its front,"[59] who marched three abreast with their stovepipe hats like "a silhouette of moving chimney pots against the last crack of the western sky."[60]

Without consulting the Governor, Colonel James Fitzgibbon (acting adjutant-general) suggested that Sheriff William Botsford Jarvis (son of Stephen Jarvis, Registrar of the Home District) take a small company of men up Yonge Street to act as an advance guard, since a strong force of between 4,000 to 5,000 rebels was expected along the road.

With 27 musketeers, Sheriff Jarvis decided to take cover; he hid on the hard frozen ground by the rail fence of the summer vegetable garden belonging to Mr. and Mrs. William Sharpe — on Yonge Street, north of College Street, near the present site of Maitland Street. (The back of the farm eventually became part of the site now occupied by Maple Leaf Gardens).

As the rebels approached, they spotted Jarvis' men and opened fire. When their fire was returned, the front ranks of Lount's riflemen threw themselves on the ground so that the second row could fire the next round of bullets. Those behind the front row, however, were only farmers and not seasoned troops and no one had explained this kind of military procedure to them. The smell of gunpowder in the gloomy night and the sudden disappearance of the riflemen's tall hats from view caused the rebels to believe that the front line had been shot down. They threw away their weapons and ran up Yonge Street. "They took to their heels with a speed and steadiness of purpose that would have baffled pursuit."[61] Lount and his men had no choice but to retreat up Yonge Street in search of the others.

The noonday sun of December 7th glinted on the bayonets of the 1,000-strong Provincial troops under the direction of Sir Francis Bond Head and Colonel Allan MacNab. Other Tory defenders included Colonel Fitzgibbon, Beverly Robinson, Bishop Strachan and Sheriff Jarvis. They marched north to Montgomery's Tavern where the rebels were hiding. The troops mounted their cannons on a hill and fired at the tavern, forcing the rebels to come out into the open. Within fifteen minutes the fight was over; the rebels fled.

On Bond's orders, Montgomery's Tavern was burned to the ground, as well as the house of David Gibson, 4 miles north, in retaliation for the destruction of Dr. Horne's house by the rebels. Gibson had been in charge of the Tory prisoners who were released when the tavern was set ablaze. Gibson fled to the United States, was pardoned in 1843 and returned to his farm on Yonge Street where he lived in peace until his death in 1864.

John Oulcott's Hotel was built in 1883, on the site of Montgomery's Tavern. It later served as a post office until replaced by the present postal station built on the site in 1936.

Mackenzie obtained a horse at the Golden Lion and escaped across the border at Niagara Falls. Samuel Lount raced up Yonge Street on horseback and hid in the nearby forest. He was eventually captured on the shore of Lake Ontario.

Two of Mackenzie's staunch supporters, Peter Mathews and Samuel Lount were hanged on April 12, 1838, in front of the jail on King Street east of Yonge.

With wrists tied and roped to each other, the prisoners were marched down Yonge Street to stand trial for treason.

Following the Rebellion, John George Lambton, the first Earl of Durham known as Lord Durham, recommended the union of Upper and Lower Canada as a possible solution to the internal strife of Canada since the Constitutional Act of 1791. The *Durham Report* lead to the union of the Canadas in 1841.

Yonge Street Murder 10

FRIDAY MORNING, July 28, 1843; an infamous day in the history of Yonge Street. On lot no. 48, in the township of Vaughn, about 100 yards from Yonge Street on the west side of the road, was a gate leading to a fashionable and well-built farmhouse belonging to Thomas Kinnear, a man who lived a life of veritable ease and comfort.

In his house lived three servants: James McDermott, a 20-year-old manservant, Grace Marks, a 16-year-old general household servant who worked for three dollars a month, and Nancy Montgomery (Ann), the attractive head housekeeper who was said to be on intimate terms with Kinnear.

McDermott was the son of respectable parents, but was a wild boy who grew into an even wilder man. He enlisted in the army, only to desert and emigrate to Canada. Both he and Grace Marks were of Irish birth and extraction and had been in Canada several years.

Nancy Montgomery ate her meals with Kinnear and spent much of her time with him, while the other two servants had to eat their meals in the kitchen and do menial work and numerous errands.

Grace Marks was a proud woman who resented the fact that Nancy Montgomery considered herself to be the undisputed head of domestic affairs in the house. Grace hated Nancy with a passion, and was often impertinent both in conduct and speech. McDermott, on the other hand, was frequently reprimanded for being careless in his work. As a result, both he and Grace were given two weeks' notice to leave the house.

July 27, 1843, Kinnear left his house and rode into town

on some personal business. His intention was to return the following day, pay his two servants and officially discharge them from service.

It was on that day that Grace Marks and James McDermott apparently planned to murder the woman they hated.

Nancy and Grace were to sleep together that night. The plan was that after they had gone to bed McDermott was to enter the room and kill Nancy with an axe.

"She (the housekeeper) was unusually agreeable and chatted as merrily as possible,"[62] said McDermott in his confession.

That night there was a full moon. The two women retired to the bedroom. McDermott sat by the kitchen fire with the axe resting between his knees, trying to summon his courage. He went to the bedroom, opened the door and saw the two of them sleeping together in the bed. "Grace was either sleeping or pretending to sleep . . . for there was a sort of fiendish smile upon her lips,"[63] he later recounted.

"I raised the axe to give the death-blow, but my arm seemed held back by an invisible hand. It was the hand of God."[64] McDermott went back to the fire and cursed himself for his ineptitude. He made nine attempts, according to his confession, and finally throwing the axe on the wood pile in the shed, he went to bed and fell asleep.

Early the next morning, Grace met McDermott in the kitchen and called him a coward. "As she muttered these words, the devil . . . entered into my heart and transformed me into a demon . . . I found her (the housekeeper) at the sink, and without pausing for an instant to change my mind . . . I struck her a heavy blow on the back of the head with my axe."[65]

McDermott opened the trap door leading from the kitchen to the wine cellar, threw the body down the ladder and closed the door.

But that was not the end of it. When Marks and McDermott went down into the cellar a short time later they discovered to their horror that their victim was not dead. She was kneeling on one knee, apparently only stunned by the blow.

He literally threw himself upon the body, placed his knee on her chest and tied a piece of white cotton, which Grace had given him, around the victim's throat "in a single tie, giving Grace one end to hold, while I drew the other tight enough to finish my terrible work. Her eyes literally started from her head. She gave one groan and all was over."[67]

Kinnear returned home on the Friday, about five hours after the murder and was told that Nancy Montgomery had gone into town by stage. Kinnear perhaps thought that a bit odd; since he had passed the stage on his way north and had not seen her inside.

After lunch Kinnear went to sleep. Following his 7 o'clock tea break, McDermott enticed Kinnear into the harness-house or back kitchen; this formed part of a hut at one corner of the kitchen. As Kinnear crossed the kitchen on his way to the harness-house, McDermott shot him through the heart with a musket ball from an old double-barrelled duck gun. Again the trap door to the wine cellar was opened and Kinnear's body thrown down the ladder. While Grace Marks held a candle, McDermott took the keys and some money from Kinnear's pockets.

At 5 o'clock the next morning McDermott and Marks were seen to arrive at the City Hotel in Toronto where they had breakfast. At 8 o'clock they boarded the steamer Transit and arrived at Lewiston about 3 o'clock in the afternoon, July 29th.

Kinnear's body was first discovered in the wine cellar by Frederick Capreol, a good friend of Kinnear, an eminent citizen and railway promoter.

The body of Nancy Montgomery was found a day later in the same cellar, ". . . doubled up and placed under a tub,"[68] in a state of decomposition.

July 30, 1843, Mr. Capreol and Mr. Kingsmill, the High Bailiff, captured the pair of murderers in Lewiston, not far from the wharf.

November 3rd and 4th of that year both went on trial (separately) for the murder of Thomas Kinnear. Both pleaded not guilty. But after ten minutes deliberation the jury found each one guilty of murder and Chief Justice Sir John Beverly Robinson sentenced them to death. McDermott's hanging was set for November 21st. He showed not the slightest sign of emotion when told of his fate. Grace Marks was to die on the same day, but her sentence was commuted to life imprisonment on November 17th, at which time she made a voluntary confession. Three days later McDermott also made a confession. He maintained that it was Grace Marks all along who had wanted to kill Montgomery and Kinnear by mixing poison with their porridge, then plunder the house and steal as many valuables as possible. "I should not have done it if I had not been urged to do so by Grace Marks,"[69] said McDermott.

He also said it was she who strangled Nancy Montgomery while he held the victim's hands.

McDermott was hanged about noon the next day, November 21, 1843. One hour later his body was handed over to the medical school for dissection.

Grace Marks was sent to Kingston Penitentiary where she remained for several years until transferred to the Provincial Lunatic Asylum of Toronto.

She was sent back to Kingston some time later, but after many petitions to the government from various sources, she was released and transferred to New York, where she changed her name and married.

Politics and Pennies   11

STATUTE LABOUR, SETTLEMENT DUTIES and occasional government grants were not enough to bring any kind of permanent improvement to the great Canadian road. So the men of Canada turned their attention to a particular system which had worked successfully both in England and the United States; this was the formation of private "Turnpike Trusts" which charged tolls for the use of the road and paid the maintenance costs from the toll revenue.

After some investigation it was agreed that such a system of tolls was the only way to keep the roads of the country in proper condition. There was, however, some scepticism about setting up private companies on the "military roads" and so an experiment began to macadamize 4 miles of Yonge Street and place a tollgate with moderate rates on the street for two years, within a mile of the town. This was not fully undertaken until a few years later, and even then it took on a completely different character and purpose.

The first tollgate on Yonge Street was situated in 1820 at Yorkville Avenue, just north of Bloor Street. Joseph Bloor was a resident Englishman and lord of the "Farmers' Arms" — an inn near the marketplace of York for accommodation of the agricultural public. When he retired he established a brewery in the ravine north of the 1st Concession road.

The tollgate was a small building with a roof extending across the road and was operated by a man named Pennock who became renowned for the fresh eggs he sold on the side. Children loved watching riders who rode through the tollgate at a gallop before the gatekeeper could get out to collect his toll. But the rider would be caught and charged on the way back.

One tollgate on Yonge Street in 1830 allowed free passage

to doctors, policemen and firemen; but charged one half-penny for pigs, sheep and goats of all ages, one penny for oxen and cows and two pence for pleasure vehicles drawn by one horse or other beast of burden.

By the early 1830s, stage coaches had to pass through the second tollgate, situated at the top of the southern hill near the present site of the city limits, which became known as Hogg's Hollow Gate.

In the winter of 1833, Kingston Road, Dundas Street and Yonge Street were improved with government loans with 4,000 pounds going to Yonge Street. This loan was to be repaid with interest from the toll revenue.

Also in that year, Rowland Burr was given a contract to improve the great Canadian road. He straightened the road at York Mills, filled the bog, drained the swamp at the bottom of the hill and made the road follow a straight line, leaving the old detours of past years as alternate roads. His work was considered a major achievement and prepared the way for macadamizing.

In 1833, a one-mile stretch of Yonge Street was to become the first section of macadamized road in British North America.

Macadamizing was a revolutionary technique invented by and named after John Loudon McAdam, a Scottish engineer, McAdam believed that the old roads were built with stone much too large and were consequently worn out by the constant action of wheels sliding all over the road. To lay a good road bed, large rocks were placed at the base of the road. Broken stone, not exceeding a diameter of 1-inch, was laid in several levels to a total depth of 10-inches. Each level of stone was allowed to settle and mesh together before a subsequent layer was added.

This technique is still used today but with the addition of tar or oil to make the road into a hard surface and prevent dust flying.

James Cull was hired to build the one-mile test strip on Yonge Street. Cull was a tavern-keeper and brewer on the Humber River, the engineer of the Kingston-Napanee Road, Deputy Provincial Surveyor and the editor of two Toronto newspapers.

The one-mile stretch of road was to be 20-feet wide, with stone 10-inches deep, with three log culverts, and was expected to cost over 1,000 pounds.

Part of Cull's estimate was based on the hope that Yonge Street farmers would sell him the stone at market price or even a bit less, and that his work could be completed by November 1, 1833. But Cull ran into problems.

The Yonge Street farmers, in order to make a profit on the operation, decided to raise the price of their stone by as much as 500 pounds and Cull was forced to travel considerable distances for stone and pay for hauling the stone to the site.

Cull received 800 pounds on account but had only finished 300 yards of the road; and the trustees refused to advance any more money until the work was completed. Six weeks before Cull was to have finished the work, the trustees fired him.

Road-builders of the era didn't realize that Canadian stone was much harder than British stone and more expensive to break, that Canadian roads curved through the forest on ground that was not smooth and packed down. They also forgot about the cold, bitter and harsh Canadian winters.

After two years of petitioning and courtroom pleading, Cull finally received payment for his work, but suffered considerable damage to his professional reputation.

What work Cull did on the road was excellent and was often described as the best piece of road in North America. He had finished two-thirds of the mile including stone bridges and 650 yards of box drains.

The trustees finished the remaining work themselves, but soon discovered that the cost for completing a much shorter and easier stretch of the road was only slightly less than that claimed by Cull. The total cost of the "Yonge Street Mile" was 3,710 pounds, or three times the original estimate.

The macadamizing process progressed very slowly. By 1836 it had only reached Yorkville, where the first tollgate was built.

Another road-builder of the day, Thomas Roy, claimed that a better line could have been built 5 miles west of Yonge Street where the hills and ravines, like Hogg's Hollow and the Rouge Hill, could have been avoided. The levelling of these obstructions was attempted but with little success.

Roy and other officials knew that Upper Canada could not yet afford such a system of macadamized roads, as most available money had to be poured into the building of canals, railways and roads in the frontier settlements. The alternative was found again in the development of tolls.

"Near Toronto, on this road is a great turnpike gate, the only one

24 The Yonge Street Radial Line

25 The original Toronto Railway horse-drawn coach.

26 Yonge Street traffic, King and Yonge Streets, 1912.

27 Northbound Yonge streetcar, December 24, 1912. The streetcars were called 'Peter Witt' trains.

26

27

in Canada. The inhabitants of these parts did not relish it at first; but now they have three miles of macadamized road which is to be extended many miles further; they are quite reconciled to the innovation. The traffic along Yonge Street is amazingly great, and almost resembles that of some of the roads leading to London (England) . . . the said street is . . . a great public road and has shorter intervals between the houses all along it than any road of the same length I ever saw in England . . . The 'clearings' extend to a considerable distance on both sides of the road; and the former arboreous appearance of 'the bush' itself, is broken at intervals by numerous settlements, occupied by a 'bold peasantry', as Goldsmith terms the pristine English small farmers."[70]

In the late 1830s Yonge had been macadamized for about 12 miles north from Toronto. The rest of the road was described by a traveller in 1845 as "mud and etceteras, too numerous to mention . . . a slough of despond."[71]

Seven people were selected, in 1836, to become the Yonge Street Trustees. Among them were Jesse Ketchum, Charles Thompson (proprietor of the stage line), John Montgomery of Montgomery's Tavern and James Davis (owner of the Temperance Inn at Finch and Yonge). They were empowered to erect a number of tollgates on Yonge Street and fix the appropriate toll charges.

Before 1840, road construction consisted mainly of chopping down trees, squaring them on both sides and placing them in the road bed. This was the beginning of the corduroy road. To help reduce the cost of road-building planking a road was developed at a cost of 525 pounds per mile, instead of the thousands for macadamizing.

After a bed of gravel had been laid on the road, planks squared on four sides were set crosswise on top of the gravel and were attached by stringers (horizontally-placed heavy timber); but this kind of road was not expected to last more than five years and deteriorated quickly without repair. The major problem however, was the cost which proved too much for private investment to handle, so Turnpike Trust Companies were established to build plank roads. They supplied the money needed for the building and maintenance of the roads and were to be reimbursed through the toll revenue. Often the tolls failed to meet the high costs of construction and maintenance, and as a result the government was found responsible for meeting the debt.

To solve some of these problems, the Provincial Government established a Board of Works in Upper Canada in 1841 to assume control of building and maintaining all roads in the province from the municipalities, but for many reasons this plan did not materialize, as neither the Provincial nor the local government was willing to take charge of the roads.

Yonge Street was placed under control of the Provincial Government, while Dundas Street, the Kingston Road and the Lake Shore Road came under the jurisdiction of the county.

The Board's appropriation for Yonge Street which was assumed by the government was exhausted in 1845. The work ground to a halt and further construction was delayed for another year while legislative approval was given for the transfer of money from the Holland Landing-Penetanguishene Road. Simcoe County merchants were forced to ship their goods by way of the Welland Canal and Lake Huron route. Yonge Street travel was totally cut off. Toll-keepers who rented their stations from the Yonge Street Trustees saw their revenues totally disappear but were granted some compensation from the road fund.

The government then formed the Public Works Commission to replace the Board of Works as a possible solution. This didn't work either, as money was still in short supply and the politicians could not act or think like engineers.

Now the responsibility for roads was divided and utterly confused. The York roads; West York Road (Dundas), East York Road (Kingston Road), Lakeshore Road and Main Northern Road (Yonge), were considered at the bottom of the list of priorities and no one was quite sure what to do about them. In the meantime, the trustees carried on as best they could.

In 1846, the roads of Toronto passed into the hands of the Provincial Government.

The government hoped to keep the road in good condition through monies collected from tollgates, but this didn't work the way they had expected.

In 1847, J.H. Price, Member of Parliament, addressed the Legislature, suggesting "that the Government should finish these roads and hand them over to the District Council (local government) free of charge. It would relieve the Board of Works of much trouble, and the roads would be much better managed."[72]

The period beginning in the late '40s to the late '50s marked the era of the private tollroad. Many corporations were formed in Canada which soon began building plank roads. The creation of joint-stock companies was yet another in the series of attempts to overcome the continuing inadequacies of many roads, including Yonge Street. The Joint-Stock Companies Act of 1849 allowed individuals to operate private companies as popular tollroads. The Baldwin Act of 1849 gave municipalities the right to have shares in, and buy out joint-stock companies and supervise their operation, if they so wished.

The development of Yonge Street during this period was not without its political intrigues. Late in 1849, the Inspector-General of Canada, Francis Hincks, announced that the York roads would be sold and that the local authorities would have the first opportunity to purchase them.

But Hincks then went a step further. He introduced a bill which gave more power to private companies, allowing them to be formed for the sole purpose of acquiring public works. The bill was passed without difficulty on July 24th, 1850, and allowed private companies to place bids in order to buy public roads — in this case, the York roads. Yet Hincks actually sold the York roads several months before the bill was passed. The only advertisement of the sale appeared in March of 1850. However, a press report dated August 17th, 1850, announced that the public roads had been privately sold to James Beaty and several friends, one of whom was his brother, and another, his son-in-law.

Beaty was a Toronto leather merchant and City Councillor; and he had formed the Toronto Road Company for the sole purpose of buying the York roads. But this was a dummy corporation whose charter had been obtained through misrepresentation. Hincks no doubt knew all about this; Beaty was a personal and political supporter of Hincks and had provided Hincks with money for his political career.

The newspapers of the day, the *Kingston Daily British Whig*, the *Toronto Examiner*, the *Toronto Courier* and *The North American* saw the sale of the York roads to Beaty as a master scheme to swindle the public.

"He may dig our graves on Yonge Street and charge double for the service, and who shall gainsay him?"[73] cried the editors of the *Toronto Examiner*.

The North American newspaper described the Hincks deal as "the grossest job ever perpetrated by a Canadian Government."[74]

With a great deal of pressure mounting, Hincks told the government that he would delay action of the transfer of the roads to Beaty in order that the York County Council would have the chance to meet Beaty's bid of 75,000 pounds. But Hincks was playing games; during the last week in September he announced that there would be an auction of the roads instead, to be held on October 15th. Further, there was no acknowledgement of the Council's agreement to meet Beaty's bid until after the "auction advertisement" was published. The Coucil had been "treated with stinging contempt,"[75] said the *Toronto Daily Patriot*.

The entire pretext for the sale of the York roads was utterly fraudulent, but the Special Session of the Council which met to discuss the matter had dissolved and a new meeting couldn't be called as the members had gone home to continue their harvesting. It would have been unprecedented to call two meetings within one month, and Warden Jacks himself had no further authority to offer a bid of more than 75,000 pounds. Jacks was the Warden-Reeve, and Chief Executive Officer of the County.

The City of Toronto had made an offer of more than the original asking price, but Hincks knew that under the law the city could not hold land beyond its corporate limits.

Hincks wanted the York road to pass into the hands of Beaty without challenge and he knew that the city couldn't bid on them, that the County could not compete and that new private companies could not be formed in time to bid at the auction, which took place on October 15th, 1850.

For the price of 75,100 pounds, James Beaty became the proud owner of the York roads.

During the first two years, Beaty made a lot of money from the toll revenue but it didn't last long. May 16, 1853, the Ontario-Simcoe-Huron Railway (later renamed the Northern Railway and now the C.N.R.) opened. It ran parallel with Yonge Street and drained a lot of traffic from the great Canadian road.

The railway was "conceived as a link between Lake Ontario and Georgian Bay, analogous to the Toronto Portage and . . . Yonge Street." Added to Hincks' problems was the opening of the Grand Trunk Railway line from Montreal to Toronto in October of 1857.

Beaty and his Toronto Road Company continued to lose money

and fell behind in its payments to the government. On September 4, 1863, the Federal Government took control of the York roads.

The macadamizing of Yonge Street had been completed by 1850 as far north as Holland Landing and was still being done on Yonge Street as late as 1865. Those who worked on the road used wheelbarrows to transport the stones and earned 75 cents per day for their efforts.

Land values in urban areas rose; new techniques in engineering and construction were encouraged; and commercial activities were stimulated; but public and private monies were often diverted from other important projects to what was referred to as "favoured roads", like Yonge Street.

There were tollgates in every direction by 1857. They were a constant source of trouble, arguments and a great annoyance.

April 4, 1867, less than two years after the Federal Government had taken control of the York roads, the united counties of York and Peel bought the York roads of Yonge Street, Dundas Street, Kingston Road and the Lake Shore Road from the government for $72,500.

For many years thereafter, tollroads were thought to be the best way of keeping the roads in good condition. In 1890, a two-horse vehicle carrying a load of more than 600 pounds was charged a toll of 10 cents; a saddled horse with a rider was charged 4 cents; and sheep, pigs or goats were charged a toll of 1 cent each. Vehicles with large wheels and wide tires, which helped reduce the wear and tear on the road, were charged less for passing through the tollgate. But public opinion was soon in favour of leaving the roads free to all, and by 1896, most of the tollgates on the York roads had been abolished.

Yonge Street Comes Of Age 12

BEFORE THE CLOSE of the nineteenth century, macadamized roads were still muddy, wooded sidewalks were unsafe, street lamps, installed in 1841, were unsatisfactory and transportation, in general, was slow and treacherous. Commercial traffic up and down Yonge Street was diverted to the new Northern Railroad and many stores, taverns and hotels along the great road lost business, and several closed out.

But the people who lived on, and nearby, the great Canadian road worked hard to improve their own lives and the area around them.

One section of Yonge Street refused to give up, and every day for over a hundred years the sound of running water over water-wheels, the constant buzz of saws cutting logs and the crunch of stones grinding grain could be heard in the valley of the great west branch of the Don River, known as York Mills or Hogg's Hollow. The three mills in York Mills were situated on a landscape dotted with houses, out-houses, coopers' and blacksmiths' shops.

Beyond the top of the southern hill, Yonge Street (prior to 1835) veered to the east as a detour down into the valley to the flats below, then crossed the Don River on a rough wooden bridge sometimes known as the Big Creek Bridge and Heron Bridge. The great road then stretched up the northern slope towards the northeast — the latter section now known as Old Yonge Street. It then turned west until it joined up with the direct northern route. This was the way that the wagons and sleighs came, loaded with equipment and supplies for the Upper Lakes.

In the valley, travellers stopped to rest at the wayside tavern operated by the Vallière family before continuing their hard journey up the northern hill. The top of the southern hill came to be known as the Toronto City Limits (not to be confused with the Metropolitan Toronto City Limits which eventually extended to Steeles Avenue).

One of the early pioneers in the area was James Hogg, a Scottish settler who owned a large number of mills on North Yonge Street. Hogg extended his property and holdings on the west side of Yonge, north of the Don River and built a distillery to make whisky. He renamed his property York Mills.

After his death in 1839, John Somerville took control of York Mills and became the miller and postmaster. Hogg's two sons, John and William, both merchants, bought their father's property in the valley in 1851 and opened a subdivision called Hogg's Hollow in 1856. The Hogg brothers were the leading general merchants with flourishing sawmills and flourmills.

Through the forest trails to Yonge Street, with heavy sacks of grain sagging across their shoulders, farmers would come to Hogg's Hollow to have their grain ground into flour. As the great road improved, farmers bought horses and hauled their wheat to the mills in wagons.

Nearby was the famous St. John's Anglican Church. In 1797, members of the Church of England had emigrated to Canada, forming the first known congregation of any denomination in York. Services were held in Seneca Ketchum's log house on Yonge Street, but after the War of 1812 the location was switched to a log schoolhouse in York Mills. In 1843, a new brick church was built near the site of the old frame chapel which faced Old Yonge Street.

In that area lived William Miller who operated a shoemaker's shop, David Boyle who ran a blacksmith's shop, and George Parsons, a surgeon.

Yonge Street later crossed Hogg's Hollow "in a direct line on a raised embankment which the ancient Roman road-makers would have deemed respectable — a work accomplished about the year 1835, before the aid of steam power was procurable in these parts for such purposes."[76]

North of Aurora near St. Andrew's College, Yonge Street followed the path of the original trail towards the east in order to avoid the foreboding ground of the Red Willow Swamp.

In the 1830s Front Street, in downtown Toronto, was just a residential boulevard with a narrow stretch of beach separating it from the water, where wild ducks were plentiful. Here, too, was the

Yonge Street wharf where Peter Freeland's soap factory stood.

The area nearer the lake was considered, in the 1850s, to be a rather unsavory part of town. Gradually the shanties were replaced by the warehouses of the wholesale trade.

The area north of the junction of Yonge and Queen Streets was a beautiful expanse of forest. Yet, lurking among the trees and bushes of the Rosedale Ravine were lawless gangs of every description waiting for the right moment to rob their next victim.

The lake front as we know it today is a remarkable man-made creation, undertaken in the year 1911. At the time, a new Harbour Commission was appointed with the power to expropriate land and issue bonds to secure financing.

Under the management of Chief Engineer E.L. Cousins, the harbour was deepened to a depth of about 30-feet. The shoreline was extended south about quarter-of-a-mile into Toronto Harbour, creating a long line of docks, channels, sea walls, grain elevators and new streets, where once only mud, slime and rocks existed.

A street called Esplanade used to be a place for "promenade, for seeing ships at anchor or for Easter parades. Trucks and trains have taken this (pedestrian) place and the lake front has receded beyond sight."[77]

Gradually, a wide variety of shops began to appear in the area on Yonge between King and Queen Street — from bootmakers and auctioneers, who usually rented the rooms upstairs from their place of business, to printers and barristers.

Michael Kane owned one of the earliest shops on lower Yonge Street — a liquor store; and it was on the steps outside the shop that Paul Kane, Michael's son, drew his first sketches of Canadian Indians — drawings that later made him world-famous as the most important historical artist of the Canadian west.

Peter Russell, who succeeded John Graves Simcoe, actually gave away the corner of Yonge and King Streets as a gift to a settler named William Bowkett.

Before the nineteenth century had come to a close, downtown Yonge Street had become a veritable hangout for would-be bargain-hunters. Many people compared it to Rue Montparnasse in Paris and The Bowery in New York. The Yonge-King area became the most important shopping nucleus in the city.

One of the most remarkable business organizations in the world at that time, took up residence on Yonge Street. A young Irishman

28 Margaret Wilson (Beattie) Eaton, wife of Timothy Eaton, 1870.

known to many as "the dreamer" had a new theory of retailing: instead of offering variable prices and long credit he developed a system of only one price and cash and carry.

His name was Timothy Eaton. December 8, 1869, he unlocked the front door of his dry goods shop located at 178 Yonge Street, which soon developed into an enormous retail, mail order and manufacturing enterprise.

Three years later, Robert Simpson, a young Scottish immigrant opened a shop on Yonge Street near Eaton's store.

Stores were springing up on both sides of the road. Once an Indian trail, Yonge Street was now a major commercial avenue. Eaton, in 1877, bought a pony delivery wagon; and six years later the company moved to 190 Yonge Street. Eaton's philosophy of life was a "square deal to everybody, the people to whom we sell, and the people who work for us."[78]

In the early part of the twentieth century, the Yonge-University-Queen-College Street area was "the chief staging area for recent immigrants to Toronto. The streets were narrow and crowded, the housing was cramped and sub-standard, the languages you overheard on the teeming streets were all foriegn."[79]

In the *Canadian Magazine* of 1913, Margaret Bell described this area as having "innumerable tumbledown shacks . . . in a state of slatternly decay on both sides of the street. You peep inside one or two. For the doors stand ajar, letting in the dust from the street."[80]

In the modern world of Yonge Street, there is the corner of Yonge and Bloor Streets — often referred to as the "centre of the universe . . . a centre for sundry and city activity. Two blocks of the slickest cash registers in town . . . Among all those gritty, gaseous swirlings in the midst of all that knock-it-down-and-build-it-up-again frenzy they find peace and community."[81]

A far cry it is from the quacking of ducks, the clucking of hens and the general noise and bustle of nearly 100 farmers who sold their produce at the outdoor market in June, 1926, at Hogg's Hollow — or the frustrated firemen of that day who found it literally impossible to answer a fire call east or west of Yonge during the spring when the roads were almost always flooded.

Yonge Street Goes Electric 13

CHARLES DICKENS VISITED TORONTO in May, 1842, and found it to be " . . . full of life and motion, business and improvement. The streets are well-paved and lighted with gas."[82]

Toronto emerged from the darkness and into the light on a Tuesday evening, December 28, 1841, when 100 gas lamps were turned on for the 16,000 inhabitants of the city. Toronto was the eleventh city in North America to have its streets lit by gas. Tallow candles and coal oil lamps set in a metal holder with a tin reflector had been the only light available to the early pioneers on Yonge Street.

The Toronto Gas-Light and Water Company, the company that supplied the light in 1841, was sold in 1847 to a joint-stock company known as the Consumer's Gas Company. Almost forty years later (1884), the Toronto Electric Light Company obtained a charter to develop and supply Toronto with electric lighting. By then, the city had a population of just over 100,000. John Joseph Wright installed the first store lighting system in Canada — 15 arc lamps in the downtown stores. The arc lamps were erected atop tall poles and could give more light than other existing lighting systems, illuminating a street for one block.

Wright was an Englishman who came to Toronto from Yarmouth, England, in 1870, and was directly involved with the formation and development of the Toronto Electric Light Company. Several of Wright's associates later established the General Electric Company.

This was the time for staggering technological advancement: in 1897 Alexander Graham Bell established Toronto's first telephone exchange with forty subscribers, and the first electric power generator in Canada lit part of McConkey's Restaurant on Yonge Street.

Today there are well over 45,000 sodium vapour street lamps in the city of Toronto.

Encouraged by the success and popularity of the horsecar in such cities as New York, Boston and Philadelphia, Alexander Easton obtained a 30-year franchise to operate a similar transportation system in the city of Toronto. The Toronto Street Railway Company (TSR) was formed in May of 1861, and opened for service in September of the same year, making the Yonge Street route the first streetcar line in Canada. A new mode of transportation had arrived, replacing the old lumbering omnibuses. The horsecars travelled on rails from the St. Lawrence Market to the Yorkville Town Hall. Those wishing to travel further north either walked or transferred to one of the stage coaches.

The horsecars were to travel at the incredible speed of 6 miles per hour and maintain a 30-minute service for passengers. The fare was 5 cents. During the summer months they were in operation for a full 16 hours every day, and 14 hours a day during the winter. Sleighs were used in winter when the roads were impassable to regular horsecars

In 1861, the Toronto Street Railway Company owned 6 miles of track, 11 horsecars, 70 horses and transported at least 2,000 passengers a day. Thirty years later, it owned 68 miles of track, 361 vehicles, 100 sleighs, 1,372 horses and carried 55,000 passengers a day.

It took about three weeks to lay the first streetcar tracks on Yonge Street. At 4 o'clock, September 10, 1861, the first horsecar, with an artillery band playing on the roof, rolled south on Yonge Street from Yorkville to the heart of the city. The trip was, however, delayed twice on the maiden voyage by derailments.

People treated the innovation with great delight and apparantly were able to remain in good humour through the many derailments. As they had with stage coach travel, passengers were always willing to give a shove, a push, or a lift, to get the horsecar moving again.

The horsecars were drawn by one horse and carried 16 passengers. The vehicles were replaced at a later date with larger horsecars carrying 24 passengers and pulled by two horses.

The driver sat out in the open, in all kinds of weather, but kept his feet in a box of straw in the winter to keep from freezing. As the cars themselves were unheated, they too had straw on the floor for warmth.

The Metropolitan Street Railway Company of Toronto (MSR) was incorporated in 1878 to provide a street railway service north on Yonge Street from Yorkville to the Town Hall on Eglinton. Riders could buy twenty-five tickets for one dollar to ride the horse-drawn streetcars.

In 1885, the MSR began to operate horsecar vehicles on a single track on one side of the road. According to the company's franchise, they were to make a minimum of four round trips a day with the exception of Sunday. The fleet consisted of not more than 10 horsecars, probably all built by the Toronto Street Railway Company.

After visiting Pittsburgh in 1889, where electric streetcars were already in existence, company officials of the Metropolitan Street Railway Company decided to electrify the cars of their company. September 1, 1890, the MSR began running its first electric streetcar at 12 m.p.h. But cold weather and heavy frost caused many broken rail bonds along the route, since the old horsecar rails and roadbed could not cope with the weight of the heavier cars. The electric cars were removed from service and the old horsecars were once again rolling up and down the great road.

Heat was provided by a coal stove placed at one end of the car. It was the job of the conductor and motorman to leave the car and help the driver quiet down the horses of the horse-drawn vehicles should they become alarmed at the sight of the new cars.

The MSR rebuilt the entire line in 1891 and the electric cars were once again in service.

With the permission of the County of York in 1894, the Metropolitan Street Railway Company (called the Metropolitan Railway Company in 1897), made plans to extend its route on Yonge Street to Lake Simcoe. The speed was increased to an astounding 20 m.p.h.

The village residents of Thornhill, in 1896, watched a crew of workers lay tracks on Yonge Street for the new radial line north and "some shook their heads and solemnly predicted that cars with steel wheels would never be able to climb the long hills on smooth rails."[83] As the electrification had not been finished in time, it was decided to attach some horses to an old Toronto Street Railway car for the journey. At the top of each hill en route to Richmond Hill, the horses were unhitched and the car rolled down the other side of the hill by its momentum.

May 2, 1897, thirteen single, closed cars purchased from the Pullman Company opened a regular electric passenger service to Richmond Hill.

Two years later, this service was extended to Newmarket with five trips daily.

The Metropolitan Railway Company was purchased by the Toronto Railway Company, which also owned the Toronto and York Radial Railway, on August 1st, 1904.

A 24.5-mile line from Newmarket north to Jackson's Point, Lake Simcoe, was opened in 1906 and the final extension of 1.5-miles to Sutton was completed in 1909 — all under the direction of the Toronto and York Radial Railway Company. The cars were built like railway coaches, long, black or dark green, double-ended streetcars. They carried passengers, freight, mail, milk and newspapers.

After 1919, the Toronto and York Radial Railway began to lose money. Many people had begun to use the automobile, or motor carraige, which first appeared in 1898 and the Yonge Street road itself was vastly improved from Toronto to Barrie, making it difficult for a railway company to survive.

It was decided at that time that the city's transportation system be unified under one control. By the summer of 1922

29 Peter Witt streetcar; northbound 'Yonge' car at College Street, June 24, 1937.

100

30 *Five miles west of Fort Frances, Rainy River District, settlers perform statute labour, 1910.*

31 *C.W. Jefferys, a Yonge Street artist*
    who worked and lived at
    the Jolly Miller Hotel in the 1920s.

such an agreement was completed, and the railway lines came under the control and operation of what was known as the Toronto Transportation Commission.

When the Commission took over, the motor bus was being introduced into public transportation service. Toronto's public transportation system was one of the first in Canada to experiment with the idea of using buses as feeder lines to the rail services.

Also in the early 1920s, the new Commission installed an experimental line of a trackless trolley bus service. No buses operated on Yonge Street south of Eglinton Avenue — only trains and not even the new streamlined cars that were introduced in Toronto in 1938.

March 16, 1930, the last radial car arrived back at the North Toronto Terminal at Hogg's Hollow as the Lake Simcoe radial railway service was discontinued. On the same day, a motor coach service began along Yonge Street, operating on a daily service from the city of Toronto to Richmond Hill, Aurora, Newmarket, Sutton, Jackson's Point and intermediate points along the route. Local service was provided between the North Toronto City Limits (by the top of the southern hill at Hogg's Hollow) and Richmond Hill.

However, this was a rather unpopular service and was only in existence for about four months. It was replaced by the North Yonge Railway which began at the unusual hour of 7:30 p.m. on July 17th, 1930, and operated from the North Toronto City Limits to Richmond Hill. This line, comprised of 8 light-weight double-ended cars, was situated on the west side of Yonge Street, although at certain locations along the way the track varied from the central median to the east side of Yonge Street.

The north-bound and south-bound radial cars used the same pair of tracks, and every few miles or so there was a switch or rail siding for the cars to pass. There was also a telephone along the route which the motorman used so he could make certain the track ahead was clear. The fare was 5 cents per zone.

October 10, 1948, was the last day for radial cars along the Yonge Street hills from Richmond Hill towards the end of the line at the North Toronto City limits. They were replaced by the modern diesel buses owned by the Toronto Transportation Commission — later renamed the Toronto Transit Commission in January, 1954, after the Municipality of Metropolitan Toronto was incorporated in April, 1953.

The idea of building a subway under Yonge Street was first proposed in 1910 by a firm of engineering consultants, but it wasn't until 1942 that the Toronto Transportation Commission made its first subway proposal to the Toronto City Council. After several years of planning the project received the go-ahead signal. On a cold, bright morning, March 30, 1954, Subway Day was declared in the City of Toronto and the first subway in Canada opened for business.

Subway cars built by the Gloucester Railway Carriage and Wagon Company of England made their maiden voyage along the original 4.6-mile stretch of subway track. The line took 4½ years to build and cost approximately $67 million.

March 31, 1973, the Yonge subway line was opened to York Mills Station, a concrete island beneath a branch of the Don River. The walls of the station are 4-feet thick, while the floor is 8½-feet thick of reinforced concrete, preventing the entire structure from floating or cracking.

On March 30, 1974, the Yonge subway line was extended north

32 Yonge Street is ripped apart to make way for Canada's first subway system.

33 *Construction on the Yonge Street subway system.*

34 *A southbound Yonge Street subway train between Eglinton and Davisville.*

35 The first subway train on the York Mills Extension, March 31, 1973.

36 Modern lightweight aluminum subway train, built by Hawker-Siddeley Canada Ltd., 1975.

to Finch Station; and by 1976 there were 9.7 miles of subway track under Yonge Street (excluding sidings and cross-overs).

Streetcars were removed from service on Yonge Street in 1954, and the Yonge trolley buses were discontinued in 1973 with the completion of the subway extension to York Mills. Only several local bus routes up and down Yonge Street have survived to service various sections of the great road.

Long Road To Rainy River   14

THE FIRST AUTOMOBILE, or motor carriage, made its appearance on the roads as early as 1898. Its presence made the improvement of highways vital.

Four years earlier, the Good Roads Association had been formed to encourage road construction and maintenance, and to improve legislation for the betterment of road travel.

By the turn of the century, stone crushers, graders and rollers became a familar sight on Yonge Street.

Motor vehicle licenses were first issued by the Province of Ontario in 1904, and in that year there were 535 passenger cars in the province, but no commercial vehicles or motorcycles.

In 1912, a statutory fund of $5 million was established for the development of trunk roads, bridges and other improvements in northern Ontario and was administered by the Northern Development Branch of the Department of Lands, Forests and Mines. This was the first government branch formed since Confederation that was involved with the construction and maintenance of roads. The fund was known in 1915 as the Northern and North-Western Development Act.

A report of the Royal Commission on Roads one year later, led to the formation of the Department of Public Highways under the Minister of Public Works and Highways.

The cost of building permanent roads in York County in 1916 was shared by the county, city and province under the Toronto and York Roads Commission.

The road north, or Yonge Street, was given the number 11 and designated a highway. The first numbered highway in Ontario was the Toronto to Hamilton route, highway no. 2, so designated about 1917.

Yonge Street as Highway no. 11 extended from Toronto to the Severn Bridge on the northern tip of Lake Couchiching, a distance of about 90 miles.

The definition of a 'vehicle' in 1920, according to the Street Traffic Regulations, included carriage, cart, wagon, buggy, truck, sled, sleigh, bicycle, motorcycle, automobile, car, streetcar or other vehicles of whatever description.

In the early days of motor travel, drivers were required to take as much care as possible not to frighten the horses on the road and to stop on signal. Speed limits ranged from 10 m.p.h. in the city to 15 m.p.h. on the highways, and drivers had to slow down within 100 yards of a horse-drawn vehicle.

According to the Highway Traffic Act of 1928, if horses were travelling faster than cars, the car drivers had to turn to the right as quietly as possible; and those in charge of vehicles could not frighten the horses.

Near the end of the 1920s, the Ford Motor Company was producing as many as 25,000 cars a month.

With the increase in traffic along Yonge Street, the Department of Public Highways created Yonge Boulevard in 1922 (west of the present Yonge Street at Hogg's Hollow) to improve the crossing of the Don River in the area of Hogg's Hollow. This new section of Yonge Street turned west at the top of the southern hill at York Mills, followed the elevated land in a northwesterly direction, then turned back to meet the original survey of Yonge Street.

Prompted by the expansion of mining and forestry in Northern Ontario and the public outcry for more attention to the frontier settlements in the north, a new Department of Northern Development was established in 1925.

The authority of the Department of Northern Development in 1926 for most of the road work was carried on under the Northern Development Act. In the electoral districts of Muskoka and Parry Sound, only trunk roads and branch roads were included in the northern development activities.

The territory was divided into ten sections with a District Engineer in charge of each district with James Sinton as the Chief Engineer.

Organization of the Department of Northern Development

1 Huntsville	Muskoka and Parry Sound
2 North Bay	Nipissing, Sturgeon Falls, North Renfrew
3 Sudbury	Sudbury and Manitoulin
4 Sault St. Marie	Algoma, Sault Ste. Marie
5 New Liskeard	Temiskaming
6 Cochrane	Cochrane
7 Kapuskasing	Kapuskasing
8 Fort William	Fort William and Port Arthur
9 Emo	Rainy River
10 Kenora	Kenora

North from Washago, at the head of Lake Couchiching, to Cochrane — a distance of about 350 miles — Yonge Street was called the Ferguson Highway, named after George Howard Ferguson, Premier of Ontario (1923-1930). This highway was officially opened for travel on July 1, 1927, to Matheson, the asbestos capital of Ontario, just south of Iroquois Falls and about 50 miles south of Cochrane. In 1930, it was opened to Cochrane via Gravenhurst, Bracebridge, Huntsville, Burke's Falls, Sundridge, South River, Powassan, North Bay, Temagami, Latchford, New Liskeard, Englehart, Swastika, Ramore, Matheson, Monteith, Nellie Lake and finally Cochrane.

The Ferguson Highway was a series of unconnected colonization roads, built at various times and later joined together and regraded under the Department of Northern Development and its predecessor, the Northern Development Branch of the Department of Lands, Forests and Mines.

One of the first sections of the Ferguson Highway was known as the Muskoka Road (now relocated as Highway no. 11), constructed in 1858 from Washago. Colonization roads like the Muskoka Road were constructed to provide access for settlers in the northern frontier districts.

In 1870, Thomas McMurray, editor and publisher of the *Northern*

37 *George Howard Ferguson, Premier of Ontario 1923-1930.*

Advocate, described the road: "Half a century ago McAdam introduced his system which formed a new era in road making, and while we cannot boast of having advanced as far as to have macadamized road, still we are highly favoured beyond many settlers of former days. By the introduction of ditching along the sides of the roads and elevating the centres, vast improvements have been made."[84]

Five years before Confederation, the Muskoka Road was finished to a point 16 miles north of Muskoka Falls which lies between Gravenhurst and Bracebridge.

During the ten years that followed, the Muskoka Road was extended north through Falkenburg, Utterson, Vernon Lake, and into the unsubdivided township of Perry just north of Huntsville.

It was extended north in 1876, into the southern portion of Armour Township as a winter road only, and two years later it reached Burke's Falls, close to 70 miles from Washago.

The Muskoka Road was pushed north in 1881 to Stoney Creek in Strong Township where a bridge was constructed. According to a report in 1883, road repairs 22 miles north from Gravenhurst cost between $400 and $500 per mile.

From 1881 to 1887, the road was extended to Sundridge. The work halted for a time as the colonization road authority concentrated on the construction and opening of road allowances leading to the railway stations. The road to North Bay was not completed until 1916 when it was connected from South River to North Bay, a distance of about 40 miles which could then be travelled by automobile in two hours.

This 40-mile stretch of road was completed in two parts, the first from North Bay south to Powassan, a distance of about 20 miles, the second from Powassan south to connect with South River, also a distance of about 20 miles. The road was later improved south to Burke's Falls.

But the stretch between South River and North Bay was travelled very little and it was almost impassable because of the bad grades, stony hills and swamps. Several miles of new road had to be built and most of the heavy grades were reduced to a tolerable road.

During the next few years, many sections of the road were regraded, regravelled and repaired.

No attempt was made to build a through trunk road or highway north of North Bay until 1912 when funds were provided for the development of trunk roads in northern Ontario.

North of North Bay, the Ferguson Highway was constructed in three main sections. The first to be built was the short route from Latchford to Cobalt. The main road from Cobalt to Haileybury was macadamized with a bituminous surface and extended to New Liskeard in 1912.

By 1925, the other two sections were constructed. Several portions of the road were gravelled between Latchford north to Cochrane (about 150 miles), and 22 miles of road were gravelled from Latchford south to Temagami. A year later the road south from Latchford to North Bay (about 80 miles) was gravelled and opened to the public.

The Ferguson Highway, by 1927, extended travel north to Matheson, Porquis Junction, Timmins and South Porcupine. On July 1, 1927, the Minister of Lands and Forests officially opened the Ferguson Highway which for the first time provided access by road to the mining and farming districts in the north. During that year, 80 miles of the highway were relocated and built through the rough country between North Bay and Latchford which included the virgin timber of the Temagami Forest Reserve. The widest part of the road was approximately 25-feet.

Roads in the Timmins and South Pocupine mining areas, just west of Matheson were graded and gravelled in 1926 and the main roads to the mines were surfaced with bituminous penetration pavement.

Timmins was the second largest gold mine in the world, surpassed only by the Rand Mine in South Africa.

Northeast of Timmins is Iroqouois Falls which is situated on the Abitibi River and Highway no. 11, and is the location of the Abitibi Power and Paper Company — one of the world's largest pulp and paper plants.

South of Matheson and Iroquois Falls, at Ramore, is the crest of the Arctic watershed beyond which all waters flow north into the Arctic Ocean. South of Ramore is the village of Swastika where a trail once led to Kirkland Lake and the world's five largest gold mines along the "mile of gold". With less than three dollars in his pocket, Harry Oakes staked a claim which developed into the deepest mine shaft on the continent.

Northwest of Cochrane, the road followed the C.N.R. tracks and was partly opened to Kapuskasing in 1926 while other parts of the road were still under construction near Hearst (about 575 miles from Toronto and 485 miles from Washago on the Severn River).

By 1930, 40 miles of the Ferguson Highway were paved with bituminous retread pavement and the highway had been extended to Cochrane.

Just north of Cochrane is Smooth Rock Falls on the Mattagami River. The surrounding district is part of the great clay belt of the Pre-Cambrian Shield extending to the James Bay lowlands.

Late in 1930, the Ferguson Highway was extended from Cochrane to Hearst under the name of the Cochrane-Hearst Trunk Road. Construction from Kapuskasing north to Hearst consisted of digging ditches, grading and covering the roadway with clay through the muskeg. The width of the roadway between the ditches was 40-feet while the width of the clay section was 24-feet.

During the last stages of construction, work progressed at a slow rate. Gravel had to be hauled over rough terrain, then loaded and spread by hand. Steep hills had to be cut down and hollows had to be filled in by horse-drawn scrapers; and in the summer months workmen had to contend with hordes of blackflies, deer flies and mosquitoes.

By 1930, 37,385 linear feet of standard cable guard rail was erected and 128,645 cubic yards of gravel were spread over the Ferguson Highway.

The Ferguson Highway, by 1930, was maintained by the Department of Northern Development, and the name applied to the major provincial highways was changed to the King's Highways.

During the summer of 1931, certain roads in northern Ontario were designated as part of the Trans-Canada Highway, but it wasn't until 1943 that the Cochrane-Hearst trunk road formed part of the Trans-Canada Highway across northern Ontario.

In that same year, the Department of Public Highways which had been administered by the Minister of Public Works and Highways since 1915, became the (Ontario) Department of Highways with its own ministers.

There were 2,977 miles of King's Highways at the end of 1931. More than 1,000 miles were cement concrete, more than 200 miles were asphalt, 260 miles were bituminous and 325 miles were macadamized. Including all the King's Highways, colonization roads and roads in northern Ontario, nearly $29 million had been spent on construction and maintenance.

Road administration in northern Ontario by the Department of

38 Rainy River Falls, 1857.

39 Noden Causeway over Rainy Lake, Fort Frances, Ontario.

Northern Development ended in 1936 when it amalgamated with the (Ontario) Department of Highways. The Cochrane-Hearst road was included as part of the King's Highway no. 11. Pavement was extended, but in most places it remained only a gravel road.

After World War II, most of the old Ferguson Highway was relocated, and the present line of Highway no. 11 follows only a small section of the original road.

The 153-mile section of the great Canadian road from Hearst to Geraldton was completed in 1943. The annual report of the Ontario Department of Highways for that year called it the "last link of the first Trans-Continental Highway".[85] The report also described it as the 'Trans-Canada Highway'.

By November 1943, 90 per cent of the grading and 75 per cent of the gravelling of this section was completed. The area west of Cochrane to Hearst in 1943 contained Cochrane, Smooth Rock Falls, Kapuskasing, Hearst, 12 smaller communities and extensive lumber and pulp industries.

Geraldton was born as a result of "Hardrock" Bill Smith's gold strike in Little Long Lac (20 miles east of Geraldton) in 1931. Today there are also lithium deposits and immense iron reserves.

The great road continued west of Geraldton, then struck a course south to Nipigon on the northern tip of Lake Superior, due south of Lake Nipigon. In 1939-40, the road from Geraldton to Nipigon was passable for winter travel with 80 miles completed.

The road southwest from Nipigon to Port Arthur (once known as Prince Arthur's Landing) and Fort William (now Thunder Bay) was constructed in 1926, a distance of about 70 miles. It was later extended to Shebandowan Lake along the Dawson Trail.

The Dawson Trail was named after Simon James Dawson, Civil Engineer, who, along with a party of surveyors and Indians was employed by the government in the late 1850s and 1860s in exploring the country between the head of Lake Superior and the Rocky Mountains to find the best route to reach the northwest.

It was a 45-mile route through the lakes and creeks west of the Thunder Bay area and followed parts of the old canoe route and portages used by the French voyageurs of the North West Company from Lake Superior to Lake Shebandowan. It followed a line southwest over a series of portages towards Rainy Lake, Rainy River and up the northwest angle of Lake of the Woods. From 1857 on, the government spent varying sums of money for exploration, surveying and improving the route, most of which was under the supervision of Dawson.

This trail and the site of Highway no. 11 from the present site of Thunder Bay to Shebandowan are identical. The present line of the Trans-Canada Highway follows the general alignment of the original Dawson Trail from Thunder Bay westward for about 34 miles near Shebandowan Lake. From there to the eastern end of Lake Kashabowie, the two routes are roughly parallel to each other but then diverge at this point. They converge again at the western end of Lake Windegustigwan and Pickerel Lake, about 18 miles east of Atikokan and cross again at Atikokan and Fort Frances.

The Dawson Trail to Lake Shebandowan was the earliest road constructed in northwestern Ontario. In 1858, Dawson made a report to the government concerning the feasibility of a communication route to the northwest. The entire road was constructed as part of a Canadian route from Thunder Bay to the Red River District in Manitoba to open that area for settlement. Dawson's report came twenty years before the exploration and surveying of the Canadian Pacific Railway by Sandford Fleming.

During the construction of the Dawson Road in 1870, the first Riel Rebellion took place. Construction was stepped up and completed as soon as possible so troops and supplies, under the direction of Colonel John Garnet Wolsley, could be moved to the Red River settlement at Fort Garry (now Winnipeg). Wolsley turned northward at the eastern end of Lake Kashobowie to Lac des Mille Lacs on his way to Manitoba.

Way stations, or crude log cabins, where weary travellers could eat and rest before continuing on their journey were an important part of the Dawson Route.

The colonization road west from Fort Frances at Rainy Lake to Lake of the Woods was first located by the government in the mid-1870s and was further constructed in 1885 to the first Indian Reserve, a total distance of 13 miles at a cost of about $187 per mile. It followed the course of Rainy River to Emo and was later relocated as the present Highway no. 602. There was also a colonization road from the town of Rainy River west to Long Sioux Indian Reserve which also followed the river but the area in between was wilderness, unconnected except for the chain of lakes and portage routes.

In the 1890s, a summer steamboat service brought passengers

from Kenora to the town of Rainy River and on to Fort Frances. The colonization road was abandoned with the coming of the railway.

Under the initial guidance and promotion of Sir William MacKenzie and Sir Donald Mann, 55 miles of railway track between Rainy River and Fort Frances were opened on October 10, 1901. The various railway companies and lines which both these men were involved in operated for many years under the name of the Canadian Northern Railway, until 1922 when they were nationalized by the government and became known as the Canadian National Railways.

With the promotion of the farming industry in the Rainy River district and an agricultural boom in the early 1920s, a gravel road was built between Fort Frances and Rainy River, part of which was called the Cloverleaf Trail.

The discovery of large iron ore deposits at Atikokan in the 1890s and later at Steep Rock Lake from 1929 to 1942, and the need for wartime metals developed a prosperous mining industry, and was a major factor leading to the opening of Highway no. 11 between Thunder Bay and Atikokan.

The municipalities between Fort Frances and Rainy River formed the Fort Frances-Rainy River Road Snow Ploughing Association in 1929 to finance and keep the road open during the winter season.

One year later, the most important highway conference ever held in northwestern Ontario took place at Fort William. The communities along the Canadian Pacific and Canadian National Railway lines agreed that the Trans-Canada Highway should be built not only from the Lakehead to Winnipeg, by way of Dryden and Kenora, but that another highway should be built from the Lakehead west to Fort Frances.

Two important events occurred during the next several years. In 1936, the Fort Frances-Kenora Highway was opened, (now Highway no. 71 and part of the Trans-Canada Voyageur Route). Three years later, the first survey for the construction of the Trans-Canada Highway no. 11 was begun from Fort Frances east to Kashabowie, a distance of about 150 miles, in order to complete the link with the road west from Thunder Bay.

August 13, 1954, Premier Leslie Frost of Ontario swung a broadaxe and cut the traditional ribbon, thereby opening the Trans-Canada Highway no. 11 from Port Arthur-Fort William, west to

117

Atikokan, a distance of 130 miles.

The completion and official opening of the Trans-Canada Highway from Fort Frances east to Atikokan connecting the two lines, took place on June 28, 1965, when Premier John Robarts cut the ribbon with the same broadaxe used by former Premiers to open all provincial highways in northwestern Ontario. This section of road was about 90 miles long, and included the 3½-mile Noden Bridge over Rainy Lake, which at the time of construction in 1958 was considered to be the longest pre-stressed concrete structure in the Commonwealth. Pre-stressed, pre-cast concrete-filled steel tube piles were barged out to the site where the bridge was constructed, at a cost of approximately $7 million. The cost of the new highway itself was close to $13 million.

The *Fort Frances Times* called this section of road from Atikokan west to Fort Frances, "the final gap in an Ontario Highway stretching between Yonge Street in Toronto and Atwood Avenue in Rainy River,"[86] a distance of 1,178.3 miles.

When this part of the highway was opened in 1965, it was known as the Trans-Canada Voyageur Route; and on today's road map Ontario, Highway no. 11 west from Thunder Bay is also known as the Voyageur Route which swings north to Kenora just west of Emo, or about 25 miles west of Fort Frances. The northern part of the Voyageur Route is known as Highway no. 71 which links up with the Trans-Canada Superior Route or Highway no. 17 extending northwest into Manitoba.

Part of Highway no. 11 was called the Voyageur Route because this was once the means of joining eastern and western Canada until the railways were built. In the early years of Canada's history, the explorers, fur traders and settlers used the Voyageur Route to the west, to the Longlac-Geraldton area, across to Lake Nipigon, down to Lake Superior and along its northern · shore to what is now Thunder Bay. They then travelled to Kaministikwia River, then by way of the Dawson Road to the Shebandowan Lakes, Rainy Lake and on to Rainy River. The voyageurs were strong men who paddled their big freighter canoes and sang their French Canadian songs while carrying two 90-pound packs over the portage.

When that section of road from Atikokan to Fort Frances was opened in 1965, the road west of Emo to the town of Rainy River was designated as Highway no. 11 and is also considered to be part of the Trans-Canada Highway according to the latest

Ontario road map and the Department of Transportation and Communication. June 28, 1965, the great Canadian road from Toronto's lakefront to Rainy River became a reality.

During the long history of the great Canadian road; sections of it had been known by many names and designations: Yonge Street, the Coldwater Trail, the Penetanguishene Road, the Muskoka Road, the Ferguson Highway, the Dawson Road, King's Highway no. 11, and Trans-Continental Highway, the Trans-Canada Highway Northern and Voyageur Routes — all a continuation of the same road, Yonge Street, first explored in 1793, surveyed in 1794 and officially opened in 1796.

The Yonge Street 'Strip'   15

THE GREAT CANADIAN ROAD seems to have survived everything from an armed rebellion to the constant cutting and gouging of the axe, mattock, pick, shovel, bulldozer and earth-mover. It even survived the onslaught of Hurricane Hazel in 1954 when torrential rains and fierce winds toppled trees, sliced hydro and telephone wires and destroyed the Yonge Street bridge over the Don River at Hogg's Hollow.

Yonge Street in the heart of Toronto has been called the greatest shopping centre in Canada, the longest street in the land, and indeed the world, but also the filthiest street in existence and Toronto's "little Broadway".

Merchandise from all over the world can be found on Yonge Street: wool and silk keshan rugs from Persia, India and China, exotic perfume from France, Rorstand pottery from Sweden, stoneware vases from Finland and blue and white porcelain from Denmark.

There are shops for bargain seekers, the middle class, the upper class, for tall people, for short people, for necktie lovers, quality shops, quantity shops, souvenir shops, sporting goods shops, second-hand bookshops, shoe stores, luggage stores, restaurants of every description. There are also "sexploitation" cinemas, bizarre boutiques, taverns, nightclubs, body-rub parlours, strip joints . . . the list goes on.

It has been described as a "flashy neon showcase of pornography . . . and department stores, of blue-denim crowds and souped-up jacked-up cars, hustlers and suburban voyeurs."[87]

When the rock musical *Hair* made its debut in the early 1970s, nudity on stage became history. At the same time, Yonge Street was literally taken over by the so-called sex trade, with the accompanying pornographic bookstores, movie outlets, featuring violence and lust, and body-rub parlors, some of which were brothels.

Those in the back streets of the city who supplied various outlets with pornographic literature soon became big-time operators in the sex trade with major connections to pornographic publishing houses in the United States. Millions of Canadian dollars were said to have been channelled into the United States.

The first body-rub parlor on Yonge Street was opened in April, 1971, by a New York publisher. One of the first pornographic film houses on Yonge Street — and in Toronto — was the *21st Century Love Cinema*, established by Joe "The Porno King" Martin.

There were 30 body-rub parlours on Yonge Street by mid-1973 and two years later, police figures reported more than 100 such parlours on Yonge Street or nearby. Store rents on Yonge Street ranged from $2,000 to $5,000 per month; body-rub parlours, sex-related bookstores and sex cinemas paid as much as $1 million to the Yonge Street landlords.

"Yonge Street will be dead in five years unless we take action now," said Mayor David Crombie. "We can and must make it unprofitable for big crime to use our city for laundering or investing their money."

The advent of the sex trade caused quite a stir in Toronto and for months the local newspapers reported on the controversy.

Malcolm Evans, an Anglican Minister, took a walk down Yonge Street with five Toronto citizens and a *Toronto Star* reporter, from Bloor Street to Queen Street, to find out for themselves what they thought of the "strip".

"To see it as one string of body-rub parlours is to miss the experience of Yonge Street. It didn't seem rowdy or in any way dangerous. It's a very human street, but it's certainly a market type of atmosphere and the market is there for whatever you want to buy."

Boris Zerafa, a city architect, " . . . we're getting a very unfortunate kind of crowd on Yonge."

Another architect, Chris Smith, likes Yonge Street and accepts it as it is. "It's colourful, it's full of people, and it's part of the character of Toronto."

Even as late as June, 1975, body-rub parlours along Yonge Street did not have, or need, a license to operate as their activities were governed by the Criminal Code of Canada. But William Davis, the Premier of Ontario, said he would be giving Metropolitan Toronto the power to clean up Yonge Street and regulate the licensing of body-rub parlours.

Ontario NDP leader, Stephen Lewis, said that Yonge Street had become a "sleazy and debauched strip, and if the Mayor and the city want to clean it up they should have the goods."

August 26, 1975, tough new laws were passed to limit the number of body-rub parlors in Metropolitan Toronto to twenty-five.

According to the by-law, effective September 30, 1976, a body-rub parlour owner is required to pay a licence fee of $3,000, while body-rub attendants are required to pay a fee of $50.

Toronto Alderman John Sewell doesn't think the by-law will control prostitution or organized crime. "There should be a limit of one body-rub parlour in Metro and Metro Council should run it."

The new by-law designates business hours from 8:00 a.m. to 1:00 a.m. Fines range from $50 to $1,000, the latter for operating an unlicensed parlour, $125 for a first offence for an unlicensed body-rubber, and a $1,000 fine for everything over the fourth offence.

A list of fees and services must be posted in every licensed parlour. Further, customers must be given a sales bill before he or she receives the services.

An applicant for a body-rubber must submit two passport-size photographs and a medical certificate confirming he or she is free from communicable diseases.

Every applicant for a license must present a health certificate to the medical officer of health in the municipality in which the applicant works.

Locking devices on doors into a room where body-rubs are given is prohibited.

Advertising is also limited. Sex cinemas are required to submit copies of all advertising to be approved by the Ontario Board of Censors. The only advertising permitted is a sign on the premises with only the mention of the name of the establishment and its address.

Arnold Linetsky, director and spokesman for the Yonge Street Adult Entertainment Association, believed that the laws were discriminatory and approved in bad faith. He challenged the by-law in the Supreme Court of Ontario, demanding to stay open twenty-four hours a day, seven days a week.

More than 30 per cent of the revenue from Mr. Arnold's

40, 41, 42 Yonge Street Mall.

Men's Club was received between the hours of 1:00 a.m. and 8:00 a.m.

"The only way to challenge the new law effectively," said Joe Martin, owner of several body-rub parlours, "is to challenge it in the courts."

Under the Municipal Act, the municipalities did not have the power to regulate business hours, and consequently the early closing hours clause of the by-law was initially suppressed but later reinstated by the Metro Council of Toronto.

Then an amendment to the Provincial Theatre's Act gave the Ontario Board of Censors control over all films and videotapes used by erotic cinemas. Fines of up to $2,000 and one year in jail for individuals and fines up to $25,000 for corporations was the penalty for noncompliance.

In answer to the by-laws of August 26, 1975, some body-rub parlours on Yonge Street were transformed into "nude encounter" parlours or "nude meditation" centres.

Armed with copies of the new by-law, James Neville of the Metropolitan Licensing Commission and sixty inspectors began their rounds of the 100 body-rub parlours in early September, 1975.

October 27th and 28th, Toronto Police and Licensing Commission officials checked the status of the Yonge Street body-rub parlours. They found 15 of 30 parlours operating without a license and nearly one-third of the parlours had closed altogether preceding the inspection. On the second day of the inspection they found 3 out of 38 parlours operating without a licence.

Whether or not the legislation can "clean up Yonge Street" remains to be seen. In 1972, there were fifty-three prostitution-related charges brought against Toronto body-rub parlours and their employees. In 1975, this number was as high as three hundred.

"Yonge Street looks sleazier today (1975) than it did three years ago when the "clean-up" outcry began. In some storefront parlours girls now make a habit of sitting in their doorways winking at potential customers. And in lighted doorway after lighted doorway nude photography, nude billiards, nude encounter sessions, nude story telling, nude meditation . . . " (*Toronto Sun*)

According to the Metropolitan Licensing Commission at least 60 per cent of the body-rub parlours which operated a year before, changed their format or converted to other sex-related entertainment outside the body-rub legislation; and only two body-rub parlours were licensed under the new legislation, one of which was a six month probabtion period, while twenty other applications were being processed for licenses.

Then came the problem of the "street hawkers," vendors peddling leather belts, candles, flowers, trinkets and fruit on the street. The Yonge Street merchants came out angrily against the "Street hawkers" calling them "tax-evading rip-off artists fobbing off imported junk as products of local craftsmen and threatening the economic future of the Yonge Street strip."

A law was passed in 1974 prohibiting the selling or displaying of goods on Metropolitan Toronto streets; this excluded the selling of magazines and newspapers.

Peter Clark, president of the Downtown Business Council, was apprehensive that once the peddlers on Yonge Street had destroyed the area, they would move shop and make Bloor Street their next place of business.

One Yonge Street venture that eventually went sour was the Yonge Street Mall. In the summer of 1971, for the first time three blocks on Yonge Street were closed to traffic and for six days converted into a pedestrian mall. Benches, potted trees, fountains, garden exhibits and outdoor cafes lined the street. The mall was a smashing success that first year.

"They should have done something like this back in 1920," said Bill Thompson, who drove a horse and wagon up and down Yonge Street for the T. Eaton Company during that era.

People rested under the linden trees, drank beer at umbrella-shaded tables, listened to bands, walked up and down the mall and met new friends.

Due to the success of the first mall, the 1972 mall was more elaborate and the third mall in 1973 lasted for 11 weeks and was about a mile long. The cost had escalated considerably from $35,000 for the first to about $200,000 for the third mall.

And the mall of 1973 was seen as a disadvantage. It obstructed the traffic and was considered to be a "scandalous and iniquitous gathering place for degenerates." Furthermore, it failed to increase the profits of the businessmen whose shops bordered the mall. While more than 50,000 people visited the mall every Friday and Saturday, some businessmen saw their sales drop by as much as 30 per cent, while others saw their revenues increase by as much as 60 per cent. Police had to be called in to contend with what they called "nuisance crimes" usually associated with crowds. Nearly

126

1,000 arrests were made.

The disadvantages of the Yonge Street Mall outnumbered the advantages. It was scheduled to run for eight weeks in 1974, but only lasted for about six weeks. The cost of maintaining it was $220,000 — 1975 and 1976 saw no malls on Yonge Street.

In the middle of all this stands the Yonge Street Mission founded in 1896 by a street-evangelist, J.C. Davis. It is sandwiched between a fast food restaurant and a tavern where bare-breasted women dance. The Mission provides a refuge for troubled men and women, offering salvation through the word of Jesus Christ, yet it is surrounded by the two symbols of North American culture — fast food and instant sex.

Happy 180th Birthday!　　　16

THE GUINESS BOOK OF WORLD RECORDS listed (1976) Figuero Street which stretches 30 miles from Pasadena at Colorado Boulevard, to the Pacific Coast Highway, Los Angeles, as the longest street in the world.

The original length of Yonge Street (34 miles and 53 chains, or 34½ miles) was longer than this; and certainly the present length of Yonge Street at 1,178.3 miles makes it the longest street in the world.

The *Guiness Book of World Records* has acknowledged this but with reservations. The Oxford Dictionary's definition of a street is "a road in a town or village running between two lines of houses; usually including the sidewalks as well as the carriage-way," and Yonge Street does not fall into this category. Yet Norris McWhirter of the *Guiness Book of World Records* says that "mention should certainly be made of Yonge Street because of its history and its designation . . . and we shall . . . as in the case of the world's longest town, Kiruna, draft a compound entry to cover both contingencies."[88] (Yonge Street is now listed in the *Guiness Book of World Records* as the longest street in the world.)

In Cobalt, Ontario, the Highway Book Shop bears the address 300,000 Yonge Street, although this figure was chosen at random.

September 6, 1975, Yonge Street celebrated its 180th birthday with a historical re-creation of 1795, a parade and a military ball.

The present-day regiment of the Queen's York Rangers received the Freedom of the City from Toronto, an old custom dating back to the Dutch wars when a military regiment was allowed to march through the city at any time, drums beating, colours flying and bayonets fixed.

43 *David Crombie, Mayor of Toronto 1972-*

The 1975 version of the Queen's Rangers in full battle dress began their march down Yonge Street from Aurora in a convoy of 34 military jeeps.

After stopping at several locations along the way as part of the historical re-enactment of selected moments in the street's history, the convoy met up with Governor Simcoe, William Berczy and a group representing the German settlers and the Rangers of 1795.

A military ball took place at Nathan Phillips Square, Toronto. The highlight of the evening was the cutting of the 4-foot by 8-foot, 300-pound birthday cake, decorated with a map of Upper Canada, 1795. A switch was thrown which activated an 11,400,000 candle-powered flare on top of the First Canadian Place tower — Toronto's tallest office building.

Two composers, Tommy Ambrose and Gary Gray wrote a song, *Long Street Winding Through My Mind*, to honour the 180th birthday of the great road:

"Long street winding through my mind
just like a picture recording time
the rich and the poor, the old and new
they built their lives and this city around you."[89]

Yonge Street was actually not 180 years old on September 6, 1975. The job of "cutting out" Yonge Street was done by Augustus Jones when Simcoe directed him to "open a cart-road from the harbour at York to Lake Simcoe". The work began on January 4, 1796, and was completed February 16, 1796. On that day Jones and his party began their return journey to York and on February 20th Jones wrote in his diary: ". . . went to garrison, York and waited on His Excellency the Governor, and informed him that Yonge Street is opened from York to Pine Fort Landing, Lake Simcoe."[90]

The work was completed on February 16th, but the official announcement to Simcoe of the opening of the great Canadian road was February 20, 1796 — the starting date from which the age of Yonge Street should begin.

Thus the 180th birthday of Yonge Street went unnoticed on February 20th, 1976.

44 One of the earliest known photographs of Yonge Street, c1860, looking north on Yonge Street from King Street in Toronto. (Ontario Archives, ref. S1191)

"When I first saw the lands on Yonge Street I found them effectively of the first quality." (William Von Berczy)

"...ladies may be able to enjoy the charming carrioling which you must have on your Bay, and up the Yonge Street Road ... where an early dinner must be picturesque and delightful." (Peter Russell)

The Yonge Street Quaker settlements were "...no Tombstone, Arizona or Dawson City, Yukon, or even a Cobalt or Porcupine. There were no girls 'known as Lou' or 'Muskeg Myrtles', or all-night gambling games during the frontier days in these parts." (James Johnston)

"O, I be (a) farmer from Markham North
And nowhere to market but Muddy York.
Me dad was a Ranger with Simcoe's men
And they blazed the old trail to the Marsh again,
'Tis Yonge Street they calls it, with stumps to spill,
But the worst of the lot, sir, is "Gallows Hill"*
(J.R.G. Adams)

"The site (Yonge Street) is better suited for a beaver meadow and frog ponds than for the habitation of human beings." (anonymous)

*A nickname for Summer Hill, just south of St. Clair Avenue.

133

Yonge Street (Highway no. 11) Distance Chart

Miles	Description	K.M.
0.0	Toronto-Lakeshore Rd-Hwy 2	0.0
0.6	Toronto-Adelaide St-Metro Rd 36	1.0
0.7	Toronto-Richmond St-Metro Rd 38	1.1
1.0	Toronto-Dundas St-Metro Rd 8	1.6
1.9	Toronto-Bloor St-Hwy 5	3.1
2.2	Toronto-Aylmer Av-Metro Rd 32	3.5
3.2	Toronto-St Clair Av-Metro Rd 14	5.1
4.0	Toronto-Eglinton Av-Metro Rd 18	6.4
5.3	Toronto-Lawrence Av-Metro Rd 22	8.5
5.9	Toronto-Bon Echo Dr-Metro Rd 31	9.5
6.4	Toronto-North York Lts	10.3
6.7	North York-Wilson Av-Metro Rd 24	10.8
7.6	North York-Hwy 401-M/C frwy Ic	12.2
8.1	North York-Sheppard Av-Metro Rd 28	13.0
9.3	North York-Finch Av-Metro Rd 30	15.0
10.7	North York-Markham Lts	17.2
11.9	Markham-Hwy 7b (Thornhill)	19.2
13.2	Markham-Richmond Hill Lts-Hwy 7 (Langstaff)	21.2
15.7	Richmond Hill-Maple Rd-York Rd 25	25.3
16.2	Richmond Hill-Bedford Park Av	26.1
19.5	Richmond Hill-Gormley Rd-York Rd 14	31.4
20.8	Richmond Hill-York Rd 11 (Oak Ridges)	33.5
22.0	Richmond Hill-Aurora Lts-York Rd 40	35.4
24.7	Aurora-Wellington St-York Rd 15	39.8
26.3	Aurora-Newmarket Lts	42.3
27.9	Newmarket-Eagle St-York Rd 5	44.9
28.6	Newmarket-Davis Dr-Hwy 9 & York Rd 31	46.0
29.5	Newmarket N Lts	47.5
30.5	S Jct Hwy 11b (To Holland Landing)	49.1
32.8	N Jct Hwy 11b-Graham Rd	52.8
34.2	Bradford S Lts	55.0
35.2	Bradford-Holland St-Hwy 88	56.6
36.1	Bradford N Lts	58.1
38.7	Coulson-Simcoe Rd 4	62.3
42.2	Fennell Cors	67.9
42.3	Fennell-Simcoe Rd 3	68.1
45.0	Churchill-Simcoe Rd 16	72.4
48.3	Barclay-Simcoe Rd 21	77.7
52.9	Painswick-Simcoe Rd 24	85.1
54.5	Barrie S Lts	87.7
55.5	Barrie-Essa Rd-S Jct Hwy 27	89.3
56.7	Barrie-Dunlop St-Hwy 90	91.2
56.9	Barrie-Bayfield St-N Jct Hwys 26/27	91.6
59.1	Barrie N Lts	95.1
61.0	Hwys 93/400 Ic	98.2
67.6	Simcoe Rd 27 (To Oro Station)	108.8
71.2	Simcoe Rd 20 (To Hawstone)	114.6
76.3	Hwy 11b (SB) Underpass	122.8
77.1	Simcoe Rd. 20 (To Hawkestone)	124.1
77.3	Orillia-S Jct Hwy 12 & Simcoe Rd	124.4
78.8	Orillia-Coldwater Rd-N Jct Hwys 12/12b	126.8
80.1	Simcoe Rd 18	128.9
81.3	Orillia N Lts-Hwy 11b	130.8

85.7	Orillia Twp Rd (C 9-10)	137.9
87.6	Simcoe Rd 38	141.0
90.3	S Jct Hwy 69 (Washago)	145.3
91.9	Gravenhurst S Lts	147.9
92.4	Gravenhurst-Muskoka Rd 13	148.7
98.6	Gravenhurst-Muskoka Rd 19	158.7
101.8	Gravenhurst-Hwy 69 & S Jct Muskoka Rd 41	163.8
105.0	Gravenhurst-N Jct Muskoka Rd 41	169.0
105.8	Gravenhurst-Muskoka Rd 6	170.3
109.0	Gravenhurst-Bracebridge Lts-Muskoka Rd 4	175.4
109.8	Bracebridge-Muskoka Rd 1	176.7
110.1	Muskoka Rd 37	177.2
113.8	Muskoka Rd 42	183.1
115.6	Bracebridge-Hwy 117-Baysville Rd	186.0
120.6	Bracebridge-Huntsville Lts	194.1
123.9	Hunstville-Hwy 141 & Muskoka Rd 10	199.4
131.2	Hunstville-S Jct Muskoka Rd 3	211.1
132.6	Hunstville-Muskoka Rd 2	213.4
133.8	Huntsville-Hwy 60	215.3
136.2	Huntsville-N Jct Muskoka Rd 3	219.2
141.5	Huntsville-Sec Hwy 592	227.7
141.8	Hunstville N Lts	228.2
142.1	Novar-Sec Hwy 592	228.7
148.4	S Jct Sec Hwy 518-Kearney Rd	238.8
149.7	N Jct Sec Hwy 518-Sprucedale Rd	240.9
150.8	N Jct Sec Hwy 592	242.7
155.8	Burk's Falls S Lts	250.7
156.4	Burk's Falls-Riverside Rd-Sec Hwy 520	251.7
156.9	Burk's Falls N Lts	252.5
166.2	Hwy 124	267.5
167.0	Sundridge W Lts	268.8
167.2	Sundridge-Paget St	269.1
168.4	Sundridge E Lts	271.0
170.0	South River S Lts	273.6
173.0	South River-Eagle Lake Rd	278.4
178.0	South River N Lts	286.5
182.7	Trout Creek S Lts	294.0
183.7	Trout Creek-Sec Hwy 522	295.6
184.1	Trout Creek N Lts	296.3
190.3	Powassen S Lts	306.3
190.9	Powassan-Sec Hwy 534	307.2
191.3	Powassen N Lts	307.9
199.3	Sec Hwy 654 (To Wisawasa)	320.7
201.3	Hwy 94 (To Hwy 17)	324.0
202.7	North Bay S Lts	326.2
204.5	North Bay-S Jct Hwy 11b (Nipissing Jct)	329.1
208.3	North Bay-S Jct Hwy 17	335.2
209.0	North Bay-Fisher St-Hwy 17b	336.4
209.5	North Bay-Cassell St-Hwy 63	337.2
210.9	North Bay-Algonquin Av-N Jct Hwys 17/11b	339.4
216.3	North Bay-Roy Dr (Cook's Mills)	348.1
217.7	North Bay N Lts	350.4
246.6	Hwy 64 (To Marten River)	396.9
270.5	Former N Lts Temagami-First Av	435.3
290.1	Latchford S Lts	466.9
292.7	Latchford N Lts	471.1

296.3	S Jct Hwy 11b-(tri-Town Bypass)	476.8
302.3	Sec Hwy 558 (To Haileybury)	486.5
306.2	Hwy 65 1c	492.8
307.9	N Jct Hwy 11b-Tri-Town Bypass	495.5
315.3	Sec Hwy 569-Hilliard Rd	507.4
319.0	Sec Hwy 562 (To Thornloe)	513.4
324.4	Sec Hwy 571-Earlton	522.1
329.8	Sec Hwys 569/624	530.8
333.6	Sec Hwy 560	536.9
345.4	Sec Hwy 573 (To Charlton)	555.9
345.6	Hwy 112	556.2
357.5	S Jct Hwy 66	575.3
357.7	N Jct Hwy 66	575.7
358.0	Sec Hwy 568	576.1
366.5	Sec Hwy 570 (To Sesekinika Lake)	589.8
375.5	Butler Lake Rd-Benoit Twp (In C-5)	604.3
383.4	Sec Hwy 572-Holtyre Rd	617.0
392.6	E Jct Hwy 101-Fourth Av	631.8
396.6	W Jct Hwy 101	638.3
405.5	S Jct Sec Hwy 577-Shillington Road	652.6
405.7	Iroquois Falls S Lts-N Jct Sec Hwy 577	652.9
411.8	S Jct Hwy 67	662.7
413.4	Porquois Jct-N Jct Hwy 67	665.3
417.7	Sec Hwy 578-Nellie Lake Rd	672.2
420.1	Iroquois Falls N Lts	676.1
428.8	Wicklow R Br-St John Twp (in L 10)	690.1
442.3	Sec Hwy 579 (To Cochrane)	711.8
448.2	Sec Hwy 636	721.3
468.6	Smooth Rock Falls E Lts	754.1
473.4	Kendry Twp Rd (L 12-13) (To Pullen)	761.9
476.9	Tert Rd 807	767.5
477.7	Smooth Rock Falls River Bridge	768.8
479.1	Smooth Rock Falls W Lts	771.0
485.1	Haggart Twp Rd (L 18-19) (To Departure Lake)	780.7
496.6	Fauquier-Groundhog R Br	799.2
502.6	Moonbeam-Sec Hwy 581	808.9
509.8	Kitigan-O'Brien Twp Rd (L 6-7)	820.4
511.5	Kapuskasing E Lts	823.2
515.8	Kapuskasing-McPherson Av	830.1
518.3	Kapuskasing W Lts	834.1
524.7	Lost R Br-Williamson Twp (In L-18)	844.4
536.7	Opasatika R Br-Idington Twp (In L 23-24)	863.7
545.5	Lowther-Post Office McCrea Twp L 23	877.9
550.1	Reesor-Post Office Barker-Eilber Twp Bdy	885.3
557.1	Mattice-Missinaibi R Br	896.6
563.6	Val Cote-Post Office Devitt Twp L 19	907.0
573.4	Hearst E Lts	922.8
575.1	E Jct Sec Hwy 583	925.5
575.9	Hearst-Ninth St-W Jct Sec Hwy 583	926.8
577.3	Hearst W Lts	929.1
589.7	Valentine R Br-Stoddart Twp (in L 11)	949.0
597.2	Sec Hwy 663 (To Calstock Sta)	961.1
610.3	Shekak R Br-Gill Twp (in L 18)	982.2
615.1	Sec Hwy 631 (To Hornepayne)	989.9
629.7	Fraser R Br-McMillan Twp (in L 19)	1013.4
640.3	Otasawian R Br-Kohler Twp	1030.5

647.6	Pagwachuan R Br	1042.2
658.8	Peterson Ck Br	1060.2
680.9	Hoiles Ck Br	1095.8
697.8	Sec Hwy 625 (To Caramat)	1123.0
707.9	Longlac	1139.3
728.1	Sec Hwy 584 (To Geraldton)	1171.8
745.6	Sturgeon R Br	1199.9
762.3	Tert Rd 801 (To Auden)	1226.8
776.9	Sec Hwy 580	1250.3
788.8	Black Sand Prov Park Ent	1269.5
797.8	Orient Bay-CNR Sta	1283.9
813.9	**Hogarth Rd**	1309.8
826.4	Nipigon-Hwy 17	1330.0
829.0	Sec Hwy 585-Cameron Falls Rd	1334.1
834.3	Sec Hwy 628-Red Rock Rd	1342.7
839.1	Black Sturgeon Rd Br	1350.4
844.3	E Jct Sec Hwy 582-Hurkett Rd	1358.8
847.1	W Jct Sec Hwy 582	1363.3
855.3	Ouimet-CPR Overhead	1376.5
870.7	Sec Hwy 587-Pass Lake Rd	1401.3
880.4	Lakeshore Rd	1416.9
889.8	Tert Rd 800-Spruce River Dr	1432.0
890.9	Thunder Bay E Lts	1433.8
892.2	Thunder Bay-Hodder Av-Hwys 11b/17b	1435.9
896.2	Thunder Bay-Red River Rd-Hwy 102	1442.3
897.7	Golf Club Rd	1444.7
898.7	Oliver Rd-Hwy 130	1446.3
899.7	Harbour Expwy-Hwy 7154	1447.9
901.7	Thunder Bay-Arthur St-Hwy 61	1451.1
903.2	Thunder Bay W Lts	1453.6
907.1	W Jct Hwy 130	1459.8
914.3	Sec Hwy 588-Stanley Rd	1471.4
917.1	E Jct Sec Hwy 590-Oliver Rd	1475.9
918.2	W Jct Sec Hwy 590-Hymers Rd	1477.7
928.1	Sistonens Cors-Hwy 102	1493.6
934.3	Finmark Rd	1503.6
941.4	Shabaqua Cors-Hwy 17	1515.0
954.5	Sec Hwy 586-Shelter Bay Rd	1536.1
969.8	E Jct Tert Rd 802	1560.7
971.1	W Jct Tert Rd 802	1562.8
988.3	Huronian Rd	1590.5
1002.5	French R Br	1613.4
1010.0	Sec Hwy 633-Kawene Rd	1625.4
1014.2	Sec Hwy 623-Sapawe Rd	1632.2
1027.6	**Hwy 11b (To Atikokan)**	1653.8
1042.3	McCauley Ck Br	1677.4
1061.2	Seine R Br	1707.8
1076.8	Mine Centre Rd	1732.9
1095.5	Bear's Pass Bridge-W End	1763.0
1099.8	Tert Rd 812-Manitou Rd	1770.0
1106.5	Windy Point Br	1780.7
1114.1	Rainy Lake-Five Mile Dock Rd	1793.0
1116.5	Fort Frances E Lts	1796.8
1119.5	Fort Frances-Central Av-E Jct Hwy 71	1801.7
1120.7	E Jct Sec Hwy 602	1803.6

1122.1	Fort Frances W Lts	1805.8
1125.4	E Jct Sec Hwy 611	1811.2
1126.7	W Jct Sec Hwy 611	1813.2
1133.0	Devlin-Sec Hwy 613	1823.4
1140.8	Emo-Sec Hwy 602	1835.9
1144.7	Hwy 71	1842.2
1156.7	Stratton-Sec Hwy 617	1861.5
1164.4	Pinewood-Sec Hwy 619	1873.9
1170.8	Sleeman-Sec Hwy 621	1884.2
1176.3	Rainy River E Lts	1893.1
1177.5	Rainy River-Eighth St	1895.0
1178.1	Rainy River-B St-Sec Hwy 600	1896.0
1178.3	Rainy River W Lts-Internl Br (To USA)	1896.3

Chronology

1783 The North West Company begins to explore new routes to the northwest and turns its attention to Toronto and the Toronto Carrying-Place.

1784 Benjamin Frobisher, a partner of the North West Company writes to Henry Hamilton indicating that a road can be built north from York along the Toronto Carrying-Place.

1785 John Collins surveys the Toronto Carrying-Place.

Chevalier Philippe de Rocheblave claims priority for such a road; and approaches Henry Hamilton for a tract of land along the Toronto Carrying-Place.

1787 De Rocheblave defines the boundaries of the territory he wants and petitions the government to grant him land along the Toronto Carrying-Place.

John Collins (acting on behalf of the Crown) meets with three Mississauga Indian Chiefs on the Bay of Quinté, to bargain for a large tract of Indian land.

1788 The agreement, known as the Toronto Purchase, is ratified at Toronto and partially surveyed.

1791 John Collins writes to Augustus Jones, stating that Lord Dorchester has given orders to lay out de Rocheblave's tract of land. Jones receives the message a year later and de Rocheblave's claim is nullified.

John Graves Simcoe arrives in Canada.

The Constutional Act (or Canada Act). Quebec is divided into two provinces, Lower and Upper Canada.

1792 Simcoe writes to Sir George Yonge saying that the military roads will require investigation.

Simcoe takes his oath of office as the first Lieutenant-Governor of Upper Canada.

1793 Simcoe makes his first visit to the site of Toronto.

Simcoe writes to Alured Clarke indicating that he intends to explore the route from Toronto to Lake Huron.

Simcoe's new town is christened York, in honour of the Duke of York.

Simcoe explores the Humber-Holland Trail, from York to Lake Simcoe, and discovers the Don Trail.

Mrs. Simcoe sketches a map of her husband's journey, indicating for the first time that the new road is to be called Yonge Street.

1794 Augustus Jones begins the first official survey of Yonge Street.

Smith writes to Alexander Aitkin directing him to make a survey along the line run by Jones, and lay out lots.

Aitkin and a group of Queen's Rangers lay out lots along Yonge Street from the present site of Eglinton Avenue to Holland Landing.

Alexander Aitkin journeys to Matchedash Bay to explore a 14-mile portage route between the narrows on Lake Simcoe and Matchedash Bay, and to survey a site at Penetanguishene for a future naval base.

William Von Berczy arrives in York with 64 German families and petitions the Simcoe Government for one million acres of land. He receives 64,000 acres, and agrees to build Yonge Street into a practicable road.

Berczy writes to D.W. Smith saying that he has only finished one-third of the road.

1795 Berczy and his men continue to work on Yonge Street, but are unable to complete the contract for finishing the road in the allowable time.

The Canadian authorities refuse to grant Berczy and his settlers the deeds in Markham and the Yonge Street lots Berczy was to receive for payment of his work revert back to the Crown.

The Penetanguishene Purchase is agreed upon and officially ratified at York in 1798.

1796 Augustus Jones begins the second official survey of Yonge Street and informs Simcoe that Yonge Street is officially opened from York to Lake Simcoe.

Simcoe's health deteriorates and he leaves Canada. His successor, Peter Russell, does not fulfill the promises Simcoe had made to Berczy; Berczy leaves York in 1804.

1797 Members of the Church of England emigrate to Canada and form the first known congregation of any denomination in York.

1789- The first settlement en masse up
1799 Yonge Street is led by General Joseph Genèvieve Count de Puisaye. Refugees of the French Revolution form the Puisaye Settlement in the area of Oak Ridges. It fails.

1801 John Stegman makes a detailed report on the condition of Yonge Street and criticizes the French settlers for being negligent in clearing the road.

Timothy Rogers rides up Yonge Street on horseback to locate farm lots for American pioneers; he opens a wagon road and founds the first successful settlement in the townships of King and Whitchurch.

1802 The "Road to Yonge Street" (between Queen Street and Yorkville) is opened and made passable, thus enabling farmers to bring their produce to the town market without having to detour.

1807 Plans for turnpiking Yonge Street begin.

1808 Samuel Street Wilmot explores the territory between Kempenfelt Bay on Lake Simcoe and Penetanguishene on Georgian Bay with the purpose of building a road for the North West Company.

1811 Wilmot completes a survey line for a 30-mile road between Kempenfelt and Penetanguishene.

1812 President Madison of the United States declares War on Great Britain.

During the war, and for several years afterward, supplies en route to British military posts are transported up Yonge Street.

1813 The construction of the road from Kempenfelt to Penetanguishene (referred to as a continuation of Yonge Street) is proposed.

1814 Dr. William Dunlop volunteers to supervise the construction of the road from Kempenfelt to Penetanguishene, but as the road nears completion, the War of 1812 ends and all the men are ordered home.

The British hold Fort Michilimackinac from an American attack.

More government money is allocated to improve Yonge Street.

1815 A new British military post is established on Drummond Island.

1816 Stumps and large roots are removed from the road but traffic is extremely slow.

1817 The last duel in York is fought in Elmsley Field, between John Ridout and Samuel Jarvis. Ridout is killed.

1825 Yonge Street extends north from Holland Landing to the Coulson Settlement of West Gwillimbury.

Yonge Street is extended north, connecting the Coulson Settlement with Kempenfelt Bay and the Penetanguishene Road, (or Yonge Street extension).

Sir John Franklin travels up Yonge Street en route to the Arctic.

Lewis Bapp advertises the operation of a light covered wagon service between York and Holland Landing, twice weekly.

1828 The Yonge Street Stage Line is launched.

Drummond Island is given to the Americans and the British forces withdraw to Penetanguishene.

1830 The government opens a portage route between the Indian station at Orillia and Coldwater, along the Coldwater River.

William Weller begins to operate a stage coach service twice weekly between York and Cobourg, where a steamboat meets the stage to and from Kingston.

1831 The steamboat, The Colborne, is built and purchased by Charles Poulett Thompson to run in conjunction with his Yonge Street Stage line.

1833 George Playter begins to run a stage coach line between York and Holland Landing.

Kingston Road, Dundas Street, and Yonge Street are improved.

Rowland Burr is given contract to improve Yonge Street.

A one-mile stretch of Yonge Street becomes the first section of macadamized road in British North America.

1834 The Town of York becomes the City of Toronto.

William Lyon Mackenzie becomes the first Mayor of Toronto.

1836 The macadamizing process extends as far north as Yorkville Avenue.

Jesse Ketchum, Charles Thompson, John Montgomery and James Davis are selected as Yonge Street Trustees, empowered to erect tollgates.

1837 Thomas McCausland begins operation of a mail line by stage coach on Yonge Street, for travellers between Holland Landing and Barrie.

William Lyon Mackenzie publishes a 'Declaration of Independence' in his own newspaper, *The Colonial Advocate*, and calls for an armed revolt against the government. The Rebellion fails.

1838 Peter Mathews and Samuel Lount, two of Mackenzie's supporters, are hanged.

1841 Toronto is lit by gas lamps, supplied by the Toronto Gas-Light and Water Company.

A Board of Works in Upper Canada is established to assume control of building and maintaining all provincial roads.

The Act of Union. Upper and Lower Canada are united under one government.

1843 Thomas Kinnear and Nancy Montgomery are murdered in Kinnear's Yonge Street farmhouse by James McDermott and Grace Marks.

1844 The steamboat, The Beaver, is built; partly owned by Charles Thompson and Captain Laughton.

1846 The roads of Toronto pass into the hands of the Provincial Government.

1847 The Penetanguishene Road or the Yonge Street Extension is cleared and made suitable for general travel.

The Toronto Gas-Light and Water Company is sold to a joint-stock company known as the Consumer's Gas Company.

A Mr. Shuttleworth begins to operate a second kind of stage coach service on Yonge Street by using omnibuses to Richmond Hill.

1849 The Joint-Stock Companies Act allows individuals to operate private companies as popular tollroads.

The Baldwin Act gives municipalities the right to have shares in and buy out joint-stock companies and supervise their operation.

Francis Hincks announces the sale of the York roads.

Henry Burt Williams operates a line of four omnibuses from downtown Toronto to the Red Lion Inn at the present site of Yorkville Avenue.

1850 The York Roads are sold to James Beaty and several friends, who formed the private Toronto Road Company.

Williams builds four larger buses which continue to operate for twelve years.

The Concord stage coach, originally built by Abott and Downing of Concord, New Hampshire is used almost exclusively on Yonge Street.

Laughton establishes a rival stage coach line on Yonge Street in competition with Charles Thompson.

Yonge Street is macadamized as far north as Holland Landing.

1853 The Ontario-Simcoe-Huron Railway (later renamed the Northern Railway and now the C.N.R.) is opened.

1857 The Grand Trunk Railway line from Montreal to Toronto is opened.

The government invests money to explore, survey and improve the Dawson Trail, west of Thunder Bay to Lake of the Woods.

1861 The Toronto Street Railway Company is formed and opens the first streetcar line in Canada on Yonge Street.

1863 The Federal Government takes control of the York Roads.

1867 The united counties of York and Peel buy the York Roads from the government.

Confederation.

1869 Timothy Eaton opens his dry goods shop on Yonge Street.

1872 Robert Simpson opens a shop near Eaton's store.

1878 The Metropolitan Street Railway Company of Toronto is incorporated to provide a street railway north on Yonge Street from Yorkville to the Town Hall on Eglinton.

1883 Eaton moves his company from 178 Yonge to 190 Yonge Street.

1884 The Toronto Electric Light Company obtains a charter to develop and supply Toronto with electric lighting.

1885 The colonization road west from Fort Frances to Lake of the Woods is constructed further to the first Indian Reserve.

The Metropolitan Street Railway Company of Toronto begins to operate horsecar vehicles on a single track on one side of the road.

1890 The Red Lion Inn is demolished. All Yonge Street stage coach lines stopped here.

The Metropolitan Street Railway Company of Toronto begins running its first electric streetcar.

1894 The Good Roads Association is formed to encourage road construction and maintenance.

1896 Most tollgates on the York Roads have been abolished.

1897 Alexander Graham Bell establishes Toronto's first telephone exchange with forty subscribers.

1901 Fifty-five miles of railway track between Rainy River and Fort Frances are opened, under the guidance of Sir William MacKenzie and Sir Donald Mann.

1904 The Metropolitan Street Railway Company of Toronto (name changed to the Metropolitan Railway Company in 1897) is purchased by the Toronto Railway Company.

Motor vehicle licenses are first issued by the Province of Ontario.

1910 A firm of engineering consultants first proposes a subway under Yonge Street.

1911 A new Harbour Commission is appointed with the power to expropriate land and extend the shoreland.

1912 A statutory fund of $5 million is established for the development of trunk roads, bridges and other improvements in northern Ontario.

1916 A Royal Commission report on Roads leads to the formation of the Department of Public Highways.

1922 The Department of Public Highways creates Yonge Boulevard.

The Toronto radial lines come under the control and operation of the Toronto Transportation Commission (later renamed the Toronto Transit Commission).

1925 A new Department of Northern Development is established.

1926 The road southwest from Nipigon to what is now Thunder Bay is constructed.

1927 The Ferguson Highway is officially opened for travel.

1929 The Fort Frances-Rainy River Road Snow Ploughing Association is formed to finance and keep the road open during the winter season.

1930 The Ferguson Highway is extended from Cochrane to Hearst under the name of the Cochrane-Hearst Trunk Road.

The last radial car arrives back at the North Toronto Terminal at Hogg's Hollow as the Lake Simcoe radial railway service is discontinued.

A motor coach service on Yonge Street begins, from the City of Toronto to Jackson's Point.

The above service is replaced by the North Yonge Railway, operating from the North Toronto City Limits to Richmond Hill.

1931 Certain roads in northern Ontario are designated as part of the Trans-Canada Highway.

1936 Road administration in Northern Ontario by the Department of Northern Development ends; and amalgamates with the (Ontario) Department of Highways.

The Fort Frances-Kenora Highway is opened (now Highway no. 71 and part of the Trans-Canada Voyageur Route).

The Cochrane-Hearst Trunk Road is included as part of the King's Highway no. 11.

The Ferguson Highway is taken over as part of the King's Highway no. 11.

1939 The first survey for the construction of the Trans-Canada Highway no. 11 is begun from Fort Frances east to Kashabowie.

1942 The Toronto Transportation Commission makes its first subway proposal to the Toronto City Council.

1943 The Cochrane-Hearst Trunk Road forms part of the Trans-Canada Highway across northern Ontario.

The Department of Public Highways becomes the (Ontario) Department of Highways.

The 153-mile section from Hearst to Geraldton is completed.

1948 Yonge Street radial cars are replaced by the modern diesel buses.

1954 Ontario Premier Leslie Frost opens the Trans-Canada Highway no. 11 from Port Arthur-Fort William, west to Atikokan.

Subway Day is declared in the City of Toronto as the first subway in Canada is opened for business.

Streetcars are removed from service on Yonge Street.

1965 Ontario Premier John Robarts opens the Trans-Canada Highway no. 11 from Fort Frances east to Atikokan, connecting the lined opened in 1954.

1971 The first body-rub parlour on Yonge Street is opened.

For the first time, three blocks on Yonge Street are closed to traffic, to create a mall. There were also malls in 1972, 1973, and 1974.

1973 The Yonge Street trolley buses are discontinued with the completion of the subway extension to York Mills.

The Yonge Subway is opened to York Mills.

1974 The Yonge Subway is extended north to Finch Avenue.

A law is passed prohibiting the selling or displaying of goods on Toronto streets.

1975 New legislation is passed to help regulate and limit the number of body-rub parlours on Yonge Street and their related services.

Yonge Street celebrates its 180th birthday, although the date is proven incorrect.

Tommy Ambrose and Gary Gray write a song about Yonge Street, *Long Street Winding Through My Mind.*

1976 The official 180th birthday of Yonge Street goes unnoticed.

1977 Yonge Street is listed in the *Guiness Book of World Records* as the longest street in the world.

Footnotes

1   Robinson, Percy James. Toronto During the French Regime, 162

2   Ontario Historical Society. Vol. XXX, 1934, 190

3   Ibid, 201

4   Robinson, Percy James. Toronto During the French Regime, 175

5   Ontario Historical Society. Vo. 39-41, 1947-9, 47-8

6   Craig, Gerald M. Upper Canada: The Formative Years. 17

7   Simcoe Papers. Vol. 1, 166

8   Simcoe Papers. Vol. 5, 176

9   Simcoe Papers. Vol. 1, 144

10 Ibid, 340

11 Upper Holland Conservation Report, 1961, 11 (John Galt, 1825)

12 Simcoe Papers. Vol. 2, 72

13 Ibid, 73

14 Ibid, 73-74

15 Ibid, 74

16 Ibid, 75

17 Ibid, 78

18 Ibid, 79

19 Ibid, 90

20 Robinson Papers. Surveying Yonge Street, 1

21 The Diary of Mrs. Simcoe, 1793

22 Robinson Papers. Surveying Yonge Street, 1

23 Ibid, 11

24 Robinson Papers. Surveying Yonge Street, 12

25 Robertson's (John Ross) Landmarks of Toronto. Vol. 3, 18

26 Berczy Papers. September 1, 1794, letter to David Smith (Surveyor General)

27 Robertson's (John Ross) Landmarks of Toronto. Vol. 3, 18

28 Berczy Papers. September 18, 1794

29 Ibid, November 30, 1794

30 Mitchell, John, The Settlement of York County, Chapter 5, 24

31 Robertson's (John Ross) Landmarks of Toronto. 19

32 Berczy Papers, 1796, answer to Administrators Proposal, 7

33 Ontario Historical Society. Vol. V, 1904, 33

34 Scadding, Henry. Toronto of Old, 1873 edition, 416

35 Ibid, 416

36 Fitzgerald, Doris M. Thornhill 1793-1963: The History of An Ontario Village, 18

37 The Diary of Mrs. Simcoe, 308

38 Reaman, George Elmore. The Trail of the Black Walnut, 100

39 Aurora: Its Early Beginnings, 9

40 John Stegman. Surveyors Letters. Vol. 32, 243

41 Simcoe Papers. Vol. 3, 58

42 Robinson Papers. Aitkin's letter to Simcoe, May 13, 1794

43 Smith's (William Henry) Gazetteer, 1799, 154

44 Robinson Papers. Yonge Street North of Lake Simcoe,

45 Scadding, Henry. Toronto of Old, 1873 edition, 499

46 Upper Canada Gazette. March 9, 1799

47 Canadian Historical Review. September 1943, 257-58

48 Ibid, 258

49 Ibid, 260

50 Hunter, F. A History of Simcoe County, 48

51 Colonial Advocate. September 24, 1829

52 Hunter, Andre F. A History of Simcoe County, 142

53 Ibid, 142-3

54 Barrie Magnet, The, August 6, 1847

55 Smith, William Loe. The Pioneers of Old Ontario, J.L. Warnica, 107

56 Upper Canada Gazette. June 13, 1808

57 Ontario Historical Society. Vol. XV11, 1919, 130

58 Robertson (John Ross). Old Toronto, 109

59 Craig, Gerald M. Upper Canada: The Formative Years, 248

60 Kilbourn, William. The Firebrand, 176

61 Ontario Historical Society. Vol. XV11, 1919, according to William Lyon Mackenzie, 137

62 History of Toronto and County of York, part 11, chapter IV, Vol. 1, 36 (McDermott's confession. Originally reported by Susanna Moodie in her book Life in the Clearings.

63 Ibid, 34

64 Ibid, 35

65 Ibid, 36

66 Ibid

67 Ibid

68 Toronto Examiner. August 2, 1843

69 History of Toronto and County of York, part 11, chapter IV, vol. 1, 44

70 Ontario Historical Society. Vol. LV111, no. 2, June 1970. (Rev. Newton Bosworth, January 8, 1835)

71 Guillet, Edwin Clarence. Early Life in Upper Canada, 541

72 Toronto Globe. July 10, 1847

73 Toronto Examiner. August 28, 1850

74 North American, The. August 20, 1850

75 Ontario Historical Society. Vol. L11, no. 2, June, 1960, 92

76 Scadding, Henry. Toronto of Old, 1873 3rd Edition, 323-4

77 Arthur, Eric Ross. Toronto, No Mean City, 234

78 Middleton, Jesse Edgar. Municipality of Toronto: A History, 507

79 Toronto Life Magazine. October, 1975, 26

80 Canadian Magazine, The, 1913

81 Toronto Life Magazine. September, 1972, 33

82 Toronto Sun. January 25, 1976

83 Fitzgerald, Doris M. Thornhill 1793-1963: The History of an Ontario Village, 71

84 Northern Ontario Roads, 1928-1944, Ferguson Highway

85 Ibid. DHO Annual Report of 1942

86 Fort Frances Times. June 23, 1965

87 Warren Gerrard. Toronto Star. May 31, 1975

88 Norris McWhirter, Guiness Book of World Records. October 22, 1975 (letter to J. Myers.)

89 Long Street Winding Through My Mind (Tommy Ambrose and Gary Gray). RCA, 1975

90 Scadding, Henry. Toronto of Old, 1873 edition, 416

Photographs & Illustrations

Frontispiece:
A common sight of the Royal Mail Stage, as the passengers try their best to free the wheels from the mud. C.W. Jefferys, pen and ink. (Public Archives of Canada, ref. C69849)

1 The routes of Champlain and Brule, Dollier and Galniee. C.W. Jefferys, pen and ink. (Public Archives of Canada, ref. C70098)

2 One of the earliest known maps of Governor Simcoe's expedition to Matchedash Bay in 1793. Copied on tissue paper in 1793, by Mrs. Simcoe, based on the original maps made at the time. (Toronto Telegram, March, 1935)

3 Simcoe named the great Canadian road after his good friend, Sir George Yonge. Yonge was the Secretary of War in the British Cabinet and a member of Parliament for Honiton in the County of Devon. (ref. 469, Metropolitan Toronto Library Board, John Ross Robertson Collection)

4 The first survey of Yonge Street, February, 1794. Field Notes, Vol. 3, book no. 366. Diary of Augustus Jones. (Department of Lands and Forests)

5 Map showing northern route of Simcoe's expedition to Matchedash Bay in 1793. Drawn by Major C.C. Bond, 1963, based on Pilkington's original sketch. (Public Archives of Canada, National Map Collection, ref. H3/400—1793)

6 Elizabeth Simcoe was the wife of John Graves Simcoe, the first Lieutenant-Governor of Upper Canada. She kept a diary of her experiences in Canada and sketched a map of her husband's exploration to the upper lakes. (ref. 4042, Metropolitan Toronto Library Board, John Ross Robertson Collection)

7 John Graves Simcoe took his oath of office as the first Lieutenant-Governor of Upper Canada on July 8, 1792. He turned the dream of building a road from Lake Ontario to Lake Simcoe and the northwest into a reality. (ref. 406, Metropolitan Toronto Library Board, John Ross Robertson Collection)

8 The first Yonge Street Tollgate, just north of Bloor Street, 1830. (Toronto and Early Canada Catalogue, Baldwin Room, Metropolitan Toronto Library Board, ref. E4:72A)

9 The Queen's Rangers under Lieutenant-Governor Simcoe, cutting out Yonge Street in 1795. C.W. Jefferys, pen and ink. (Public Archives of Canada, ref. C73665)

10 William Von Berczy was a painter, architect, engineer, and businessman. He was contracted by Simcoe, in 1794, to open Yonge Street from York to Holland Landing. He also erected the first sawmill and grist-mill in the part of York known as the German Mills. (Self-portrait, c. 1800-05; The William Berczy Study)

11 Sir John Franklin was a distinguished navigator and explorer who journeyed up Yonge Street in 1825 en route to the Arctic. (ref. 21, Metropolitan Toronto Library Board, John Ross Robertson Collection)

12 William Lyon Mackenzie was the first Mayor of Toronto in 1834. Three years later he led an armed revolt on the city but was defeated. (ref. 363, Metropolitan Toronto Library Board, John Ross Robertson Collection)

13 The John Thompson omnibus. (Toronto Transit Commission, ref. 15536)

14 William Botsford Jarvis was the Sheriff of the Home District in York and commanded a regiment of militia during the Rebellion of 1837. (ref. 899, Metropolitan Toronto Library Board, John Ross Robertson Collection)

15 The William Weller Stage Line, 1830. (John Ross Robertson Collection (ref. JRR 888)

16 Henry Burt Williams' omnibus of 1849, operated every 10 minutes from the St. Lawrence Market, and Yonge and King Streets, to the Red Lion Hotel, Yorkville. (John Ross Robertson Collection, Metropolitan Toronto Library Board)

17 The Toronto Street Railway, covered sleigh, 1861-1891. (Toronto Transit Commission, ref. 10465)

18 The first two-horse open car in Toronto. (Toronto Transit Commission, ref. 10463)

19 Robert Simpson opened a shop on Yonge Street near Eaton's store in 1872. (Archives; The Robert Simpson Company)

20 Timothy Eaton was 31 years old when this photograph was taken in 1865. He opened a drygoods shop on Yonge Street in 1869. (Archives; Eaton's of Canada)

21 The Henry Burt Williams omnibus, 1850, at the Red Lion Hotel. This was one of the four, 10-passenger omnibuses operated between downtown Toronto and Yorkville, 1850-1862. (John Ross Robertson Collection, Metropolitan Toronto Library Board.)

22 The John Thompson Stage at Richmond Hill, in front of the Dominion Hotel, 1896. (Toronto Transit Commission ref. 9005)

23 Yonge and Adelaide Streets, looking north, Pretoria Day, June 5, 1901. (Archives of Ontario, ref. S1244)

24 The Yonge Street Radial Line ran from the CPR crossing just north of Bloor Street to York Mills. It was extended in 1899 to Newmarket and in 1904 to Jackson's Point. The last radial car ran up Yonge Street in 1948. (North York Historical Society, ref. 2)

25 The original Toronto Railway horse-drawn coach. (Toronto Transit Commission, ref. 5052)

26 Yonge Street traffic, King and Yonge Streets, 1912. (Toronto and Early Canada Catalogue, Baldwin Room, Metropolitan Library Board, ref. X61-60)

27 Northbound Yonge streetcar (north of Queen Street), December 24, 1924, Christmas shoppers and Holiday traffic. The streetcars were known as 'Peter Witt' trains, in service from 1921 to 1954. (Toronto Transit Commission, ref. 3630)

28 Margaret Wilson (Beattie) Eaton, wife of Timothy Eaton, 1870. (Archives; Eaton's of Canada)

29 Peter Witt streetcar; northbound 'Yonge' car at College Street, June 24, 1937. (Toronto Transit Commission, ref. 12009)

30 Five miles west of Fort Frances, Rainy River District, 1910, settlers perform their required statute labour duties. It is not known whether this was part of Yonge Street, but the scene would be similar. (ref. 6693 S11449, Ontario Archives)

31 C.W. Jefferys, a Yonge Street artist, worked and lived with a friend at the Jolly Miller Hotel in the early 1920s. He sketched the famous "Cutting out of Yonge Street, 1795" drawing. (Ontario Archives, ref. S10204)

32 Yonge Street is ripped apart to make way for Canada's first subway system. The early stage of construction began September 8, 1949. (Toronto Transit Commission)

33 Construction on the Yonge Street subway system. Exact location and date is not known. (Toronto Transit Commission, ref. y-4)

34 A southbound Yonge Street subway train between Eglinton and Davisville. In the background are the office buildings and apartments at Yonge and Eglinton, where Yonge Street stopped in 1794. (Toronto Transit Commission)

35 The first subway train on the York Mills Extension, March 31, 1973. The train is leaving the Eglinton station with dignitaries aboard. Toronto Transit Commission, ref. A-7)

36 Modern lightweight aluminum subway train. Built by Hawker-Siddeley Canada Ltd., 1975 (Toronto Transit Commission)

37 North of Washago, at the head of Lake Couchiching, to Cochrane — a distance of about 350 miles — Yonge Street was called the Ferguson Highway, named after George Howard Ferguson, Premier of Ontario 1923-1930. (ref. S322, Ontario Archives)

38 Rainy River Falls, 1857. Fort Frances was established by the Hudson's Bay Company in 1822 and in the foreground is an Indian encampment. (ref. 2383, Metropolitan Toronto Library Board, John Ross Robertson Collection)

39 Noden Causeway over Rainy Lake, Fort Frances, Ontario. (Ministry of Industry and Tourism, ref. 4-E-1365)

40 Yonge Street Mall, Toronto Ontario. (Ministry of Industry and Tourism, ref. 720712102)

41 Yonge Street Mall, Toronto, Ontario. (Ministry of Industry and Tourism, ref. 72071213)

42 Yonge Street Mall, Toronto, Ontario. (Ministry of Industry and Tourism, ref. 72071187)

43 David Crombie was elected Mayor of Toronto in 1972. (A Cavouk Portrait, The Colonnade, 131 Bloor Street W., Toronto.)

44 One of the earliest known photographs of Yonge Street, c1860, looking north on Yonge Street from King Street in Toronto. (Ontario Archives, ref. S1191)

Acknowledgements

Archives of Ontario, Toronto

Bathurst Heights Public Library, Toronto

City Hall Archives Library, Toronto

City Hall Municipal Library, Toronto

John Robert Colombo

Department of Industry and Tourism of Ontario

Department of Lands and Forests, Queen's Park, Toronto

Donald Jones, author (columnist and historian)

Thomas Fisher Rare Book Library, Toronto

Forest Hill Public Library, Toronto

George L. Cassidy, Haileybury, Ontario (historian)

Roy V. Henderson, Toronto City Clerk

Mayor David Crombie

Metropolitan Toronto Central Library, Toronto Room, Baldwin Room

Metropolitan Toronto Police Headquarters

Mike Filey, author (columnist and historian)

Ministry of Transportation and Communications, Toronto

North York Historical Society, Toronto

Joseph Patrick, rare book dealer

Public Archives of Canada, Ottawa

Ontario Historical Society, Toronto

John Roberts Library, Toronto

Carl F. Schubring. Fort Frances, Ontario (former editor of the Fort Frances Times, historian)

Simcoe Archives, Minesing, Ontario

The Chronicle Journal, Thunder Bay

The Downtown Business Council, Toronto

The Fort Frances Times, Fort Frances

The German Canadian Council for the Arts

The Guiness Book of World Records

The Highway Book Shop, Cobalt, Ontario

The Metropolitan Toronto Licensing Commission

The North Bay Nugget, North Bay

The Northern Times, Kapuskasing

The Simcoe Foundation, Toronto

The Toronto Globe and Mail

The Toronto Star

The Toronto Sun

The Toronto Transit Commission

Tommy Ambrose, Gary Gray, RCA of Canada

United Empire Loyalists Association of Canada, Toronto

University of Toronto Library

Willowdale Public Library, Toronto

Bibliography

Periodicals & Magazines

Aurora: Its Early Beginnings. by James Johnston; second edition, Aurora and District Historical Society, 1972

The Back Fifty. DHO 50th Anniversary, 1916-1966 (Ontario Motor League)

Canada's Adventure Tours from the Trans-Canada (Ontario Motor League)

Canadian Geographic Journal Vol. XV1. no. 4 April 1938 and Vol. XXII, no. 4, October 1941

Canadian Historical Review. Yonge Street and the North West Company, by Percy James Robinson. September 1943

The Canadian Journal, 1876-1878, Vol. 15, New Series; Copp Clark Publishing Company, 1876. (Legislative Library, Queen's Park)

The Canadian Magazine, 1913

Canadian Motorist Magazine. September 1920 (Ontario Motor League)

Canadian Motorist Magazine. Vol. 14, September 1927 (Ontario Motor League)

The Canadian Motorist. It's a Mad Mad Mad Mad Street (article on Bloor Street), by Douglas Marshall. February 1975

Canadian Motorist Magazine. Main Street Canada, by Jock Carroll. April 1976

Carved From the Forest: A History of Kapuskasing by Margaret Paterson; The Northern Times Limited. 1967

Century, 1867-1967, Toronto Daily Star; week of February 13th, 1967. The Canadian Saga.

Distance Table. King's and Secondary Highways. Ministry of Transportation and Communications; 1976, Highway no. 11. ppg. 27-33

Emeritus (Historical Journal of the University of Western Ontario). The Yonge Street Area. by James Smith; Spring 1965

First Parliament of Upper Canada. Niagara Upper Canada: 1792, by Janet Carnochan (Legislative Library, Queen's Park)

Highway no. 11 Official Opening Souvenir Supplement of the Daily Bulletin; Fort Frances Times, June 28. 1965

National Geographic Magazine. Canada's Dowager Learns to Swing (article on Toronto), by Ethel Starbird. August 1975

Ontario. Champlain Country. Department of Tourism and Information

Ontario Historical Society. Historical Notes on Yonge Street, by L. Teefy. Vol. V, 1904

Ontario Historical Society. The Nottawasaga River Route. by G.K. Mills. Vol. V111, 1907

Ontario Historical Society. Annals of an Old Post Office on Yonge Street, by Mathew Teefy. Vol. X111, 1915

Ontario Historical Society. A Contemporary Account of the Rebellion of 1837 by George Coventry; vol. XV11, 1919

Ontario Historical Society. Dundas Street and Other Canadian Roads, by W.H. Breithaupt. Vol. XX1, 1924

Ontario Historical Society. Upper Canada in 1794; A synopsis of John C. Ogden's Tour, notes by W.P. Mustard. Vol. XX1, 1924

Ontario Historical Society. The Story of Toronto, by T.A. Reed; and Toronto: How and Why It Grew, by A.H. Young. Vol. XXX, 1934

Ontario Historical Society. Papers and Records, vol. 39-41, 1947-1949; The Toronto Carrying Place and the Toronto Purchase by Percy James Robinson. (Legislative Library, Queen's Park)

Ontario Historical Society. Colonization of Roads, 1850-1867, by George W. Spragge. Vol. XL1X, no. 1, 1957

Ontario Historical Society. Maps of Upper Canada, 1800-1864, by C.F. Whebell. Vol. XL1X, no. 3, 1957

Ontario Historical Society. Lands and Policies: Land Alienation During the First Century of Settlement in Ontario, by J. Howard Richards. Vol. L, no. 4, 1958

Ontario Historical Society. King Township, York County, 1800-1867: A Historical Sketch, by Mary E. Garbutt. Vol. L11, no. 2, June 1960

Ontario Historical Society. The First Great Fire of 1849, by F.H. Armstrong. Vol. L111, no. 3, September 1961

Ontario Historical Society. An Early Settlement on St. Joseph Island, by Fred C. Hamil. Vol. L111, no. 4, December 1961

Ontario Historical Society. Stormy History of York Roads, 1833-1865, by Michael S. Cross. Vol. L1V, no. 1, March 1962

Ontario Historical Society. William Von Berczy, by Lita-Rose Betcherman. Vol. LV11, no. 2, June 1965

Ontario Historical Society. Toronto's First Railway, by F.H. Armstrong; and Simcoe Settlers, 1834-1835, by Daniel J. Brock. Vol. LV111, no. 1, March 1966

Ontario Historical Society. Rev. Newton Bosworth — Pioneer Settler on Yonge Street, by F.H. Armstrong. Vol. LV111, no. 3, September 1966

Ontario Historical Society. Yonge Street Politics — 1828-1832, by Audrey Saunders Miller. Vol. LX11, no. 2, June 1970

The Star Weekly. The TTC's Sentimental Journey. A Streetcar Named Nostalgia, by Jeremy Ferguson. July 12-19, 1975

Toronto and York Roads Commission, Report of 1926. Toronto and York Roads Commission, Toronto, 1926. (Legislative Library, Queen's Park)

Toronto Life. Toronto's First Foreigners, by Robert Harney and Harold Troper. October 1975

Toronto Month. A Lake Simcoe Tour; October 3-November 6, 1975

The Toronto Star Souvenir Supplement. Historic section. How the Harbor Reformed Tawdry Toronto, by Hyman Solomon. June 27th 1959

Traveller's Encyclopedia of Ontario. Ministry of Industry and Tourism

Turnpikes . . . Roads in Canada. by Irma Pattison; DHO News, September 1963. (Ontario Motor League)

The Upper Holland Conservation Report. Department of Planning and Development; Toronto, 1953. (Queen's Park Legislative Library)

York Pioneer and Historical Society. Historic Yonge Street, by Vivian Wilcox, 1932; and the York Pioneer 1964, Gallows Hill Poem

Manuscripts & Government Documents

A Plan For Ontario Highways; Engineering Analysis of Needs of King's Highways and Secondary Roads; Ontario Department of Highways, Toronto, 1956. (City Hall Municipal Library)

Accessibility and Rural Land Utilization in the Yonge Street Area of Upper Canada. By T.F. McIlwraith, University of Toronto Thesis, 1966. (Thomas Fisher Rare Book Library)

Chronology, 1792-1830. Principal Roads Prior to Toll Roads; Government Records, Department of Transportation and Communications Historical Collection (old DHO) (Archives of Ontario)

Creation of a Pedestrian Mall on Yonge Street. Toronto, 1970. (City Hall Municipal Library)

Crown Lands on Yonge Street. Audrey Saunders. (Toronto Central Library, Baldwin Room)

Diary of T.H. Ware. Journey to Orillia; 1844. (Simcoe County Archives)

Field Notes, Vol. 1, 1793, ppg. 251-254. The Diary of Alexander Aitkin. (Department of Lands and Forests)

Field Notes, Vol. 2, no. 355-358; 1793. Alexander Aitkin. (Department of Lands and Forests)

Field Notes, Vol. 3, book no. 366; 1793-4 Diary of Augustus Jones. (Department of Lands and Forests)

Highway Construction Program, King's and Secondary Highway Construction; Ontario Department of Highways, no date. (City Hall Municipal Library)

Historical Chronology of Highway Legislation in Ontario, 1774-1961; Ontario Department of Highways. (Legislative Library, Queen's Park)

History of Early Road Grants in Upper Canada. Prepared by Miss Gamey of the Northern Development Branch, Ontario Government, 1937. (Archives of Ontario)

Index, Ontario Roads, 1851-1901, Book 11. Government Records, Department of Transportation and Communications Historical Collection (old DHO). (Archives of Ontario)

Indian Trails; New York to Ontario. Government Records, Department of Transportation and Communications Historical Collection (old DHO) (Archives of Ontario)

Legislative History of Road and Bridge Administration in Ontario. Irma Pattison; Toronto, April 1969. (Legislative Library, Queen's Park)

The Moore Scrapbooks, approximately 1948-1950. (Simcoe County Archives)

Northern Ontario Roads, 1928-1944. Government Records, Department of Transportation and Communications Historical Collection (old DHO). (Archives of Ontario)

Ontario Highways: Their Origin, Development and present Trends in Location and Design; Ontario Department of Highways, no date. (City Hall Municipal Library)

Report of the Department of Public Records and Archives of Ontario, 1929, by Alexander Fraser. Printed by order of the Legislative Assembly of Ontario. Sessional Paper 26, 1930. (Archives of Ontario)

Report of Public Roads and Highways Commission. Toronto King's Press; Toronto 1914

Roads and Streets, Facts and Figures on Highway Construction. Canadian Good Roads Association; Ottawa, March 1954. (Legislative Library, Queen's Park)

Simcoe's Yonge Street, by Percy James Robinson. An unpublished Account of Simcoe's First Exploration of the Yonge Street Route, no date. (Thomas Fisher Rare Book Library)

Studies in Yonge Street Settlement based on the O'Brian Diary, by Audrey Murton Saunders. University of Toronto Thesis, 1944. (Thomas Fisher Rare Book Library)

Surveyors' Letters, Vol. 9, no. 4,5,6; 1797. Alexander Aitkin. (Department of Lands and Forests)

Surveyors Letters, Vol. 6, ppg. 1902, 1904, 1896; 1797. Augustus Jones. (Department of Lands and Forests) Surveyors' letters, Vol. 28, no. 67, 131, 135; 1795 Augustus Jones. (Department of Lands and Forests)

Surveyors' Letters, Vol. 4, no 1138-1139; 1795. D. W. Smith. (Department of Lands and Forests)

Surveyors' Letters Received, Vol. 9, no. 621, 622; 1799. D. W. Smith and William Chewett. (Department of Lands and Forests)

Surveyors' Letters, Vol. 32, ppg. 243, 167; 1801. John Stegman. (Department of Lands and Forests)

Surveyors' Letters, Vol. 42, ppg. 162-163; 1801. John Stegman. (Department of Lands and Forests)

Township of York Historical Series. Vol. 2, 1975. Edited by Ivar Hiessler; Transportation, 1840-1900 by Paul Sentesy. Social and Cultural Development. (1820-1900) by Kristine Black. (Roberts Library)

Transportation on Yonge Street. A History; Toronto, 1973. (City Hall Municipal Library)

Upper Holland Valley Conservation Report. Land Forest; 1961. Ontario Department of Commerce and Development. (Legislative Library, Queen's Park)

Upper Holland Valley Conservation Report. Water; 1966. Department of Energy and Resources Management. (Legislative Library, Queen's Park)

The Yonge Street Area. University of Western Ontario Thesis; J.E. Smith, London, Ontario, 1963

Yonge Street Mall: A Feasibility Study; The City People, Community Planning and Research Incorporated; Toronto, 1974. (City Hall Municipal Library)

Yonge Street Mall. Development, Research and Information Division; Toronto, 1971. (City Hall Municipal Library)

Yonge Street Pedestrian Mall. William Archer (miscellaneous papers); Toronto, 1972. (City Hall Municipal Library)

Transit in Toronto, Toronto Transit Commission, first printing, 1967; revised, 1976

Papers & Letters

The Berczy Papers. (Archives of Ontario)

The Robinson (Percy James) Papers. An unpublished MANUSCRIPT OF Simcoe's Yonge Street, 1793-1796. No date. (Archives of Ontario)
sections:
Exploring Yonge Street
Surveying Yonge Street
Yonge Street and Holland Landing
York, 1793-4
York, 1794-5
York, 1795-6
North of Lake Simcoe
William Berczy
On Toronto

The Robinson (Percy James) Papers. Yonge Street a) to the war of 1812; b) 1814-1937; Historic Roads Series. CBC Radio, May 10th-June 28th, 1937. This copy of Robinson's script for the broadcast on Yonge Street was made by Mr. Cook of the Ontario Department of Highways, August, 1938. (Archives of Ontario)

Russell Papers. Vol. 2, 1797-1798. Collected and edited by Brigadeer General E.A. Cruikshank; The Ontario Historical Society; Toronto, 1935. (City Hall Archives)

Russell Papers. Vol. 3, 1798-1799. Ontario Historical Society; Toronto, 1936. (City Hall Archives)

Simcoe Papers. Vol. 1, 1789-1793. Collected and edited by Brigadeer General E.A. Cruikshank. The Ontario Historical Society. Toronto, 1923. (City Hall Archives)

Simcoe Papers, Vol. 2, 1793-1794. Ontario Historical Society; Toronto, 1924 (City Hall Archives)

Simcoe Papers, Vol. 3. 1794-1795. Ontario Historical Society; Toronto, 1925 (City Hall Archives)

Simcoe Papers, Vol. 4, 1795-1796. Ontario Historical Society; Toronto, 1926 (City Hall Archives)

Letter to Jay Myers from Roy V. Henderson, Toronto City Clerk. January 22, 1976. (Information concerning the September 6, 1975 Yonge Street birthday celebration)

Letter to Jay Myers from Douglas Pollard, Highway Book Shop. January 11, 1975 (Information on 300,000 Yonge Street)

Letter to Jay Myers from Colleen Walsh for L. Kelly, Managing Director of the Downtown Business Council. February 17, 1976. (Information concerning the September 6, 1975 Yonge Street birthday celebration)

Letter to Jay Myers from Norris McWhirter, Guiness Book of World Records. October 22, 1975

Letter to Sir Joseph Banks (president of Royal Society of Great Britain), 1791; written by John Graves Simcoe (Legislative Library, Queen's Park)

Miscellaneous

Historical Atlas of Simcoe County, Ontario (Illustrated);
H. Belden and Company, 1881. (Reprinted by Cumming
Atlas Reprints, Port Elgin, 1975)

Illustrated Historical Atlas of the County of York. Selected
and reprinted from the original 1878 edition; Peter
Martin Associates, 1969.

The Municipality of Metropolitan Toronto By-law no.
137-75 and 88-69; Metropolitan Licensing Commission

Record. Long Street Winding Through My Mind. Music
by Tommy Ambrose, lyrics by Gary Gray. RCA recording.
Sunbury Music Canada Limited (CAPAC PB-50117-B), 1975

Books

A Short Topographical Description of His Majesty's
Province of Upper Canada in North America; Johnson
Reprint Corporation, 1969. (originally published by W.
Faden, Charing Cross, 1799.) (Toronto Central Library,
Baldwin Room)

Adam, Graeme Mercer. Toronto, Old and New; Mail
Printing Company, Toronto 1891.

Andre, John. Infant Toronto as Simcoe's Folly; Cen-
tennial Press, Toronto, 1971

Arthur, Eric Ross. Toronto, No Mean City; University
of Toronto Press; Toronto, 1964

Campbell, Marjorie Wilkins; Ontario; Ryerson Press,
Toronto, 1953

Canniff, William. The Settlement of Upper Canada;
Mika Silk Screening, Belleville Ontario, 1971. (Originally
published in 1869 by Dudley & Burns, Toronto)

Colombo, John Robert. Colombo's Canadian Quotations;
Hurtig, Edmonton, 1974

Craig, Gerald M. Early Travellers in the Canadas, 1791-1867;
selected and edited by Gerald M. Craig; Macmillan
(Canada) Toronto, 1955

Craig, Gerald M. Upper Canada; The Formative Years,
1784-1841; McClelland and Stewart, Toronto, 1963

DeVolpi, Charles Patrick. Toronto; a Pictorial Record;
Dev-Sco Publications, Montreal, 1965

Duff, James Clarence. Pen Sketches of Historic Toronto
published by the author; Toronto, 1967. (Vol.s 1 and 2)

Filey, Michael. Passengers Must Not Ride On Fenders;
Green Tree Publications, Toronto, 1974

Firth, Edith. The Town of York, 1793-1815; Champlain
Society, Toronto Publications, Ontario Series, 5, 1962

Firth, Edith. The Town of York, 1815-1834; Champlain
Society, Toronto Publications, Ontario Series 8, 1966

Fitzgerald, Doris M. Thornhill 1793-1963; the History
of An Ontario Village, Thornhill, 1964

Gilbert, John and Duncan P. Read. Collier-Macmillan,
Toronto, 1972

Glazebrook, George Parger de Tenebroker. The Story
of Toronto; University of Toronto Press, Toronto, 1971

Graham, Audrey. 150 Years at St. John's York Mills;

General Publishing Company, Toronto, 1966

Guillet, Edwin Clarence. Early Life in Upper Canada;
Vol. 3; Ontario Publishing Company, Toronto 1958

Guillet, Edwin Clarence. Pioneer Days in Upper Canada;
University of Toronto Press, Toronto 1964

Guillet, Edwin Clarence. Pioneer Inns and Taverns,
vol. 3; Ontario Publishing Company, Toronto 1958

Guillet, Edwin Clarence. Pioneer Settlements in Upper
Canada; University of Toronto Press, Toronto 1969

Guillet, Edwin Clarence. Pioneer Travel in Upper Canada;
University of Toronto Press, Toronto, 1966

Hale, Katherine. Toronto: Romance of a Great City;
Cassell and Company Limited, Toronto, 1965

Handbook of Toronto. by a member of the Press;
Lovell and Gibson Publishing Company, Toronto, 1858
(City Hall Archives)

Hart, Patricia. Pioneering in North York; General Publishing Company, Toronto 1968

History of Toronto and County of York, Vol. 1. C. Blackett
Robinson Publishing Company, Toronto, 1885 (Robarts
Library)

Hounson, Eric Wilfrid. Toronto in 1810; Ryerson Press,
Toronto, 1970

Hunter, Andre F. A History of Simcoe County, Vol. 1:
Published by the County Council, Barrie Ontario, 1909.
Reproduced edition by Martha Hunter, Warwick Bros.
and Rutter Ltd., Toronto, 1948.

Jarrett, Gordon. Metropolitan Toronto Past and Present;
D.B. Kirkup, Toronto, 1973

Judd, W. A Naturalist's Guide to Ontario, edited by
W. Judd and J. Murray Speirs; University of Toronto
Press, Toronto, 1964

Kerr, Donald. The Changing Face of Toronto — a study
in Urban Geography by Donald Kerr and Joseph Spelt;
Queen's Printer, Ottawa, 1967

Kilbourn, William. The Firebrand; William Lyon Mackenzie
and the Rebellion in Upper Canada; Clarke Irwin, Toronto,
1964

Kurelek, William. O Toronto; New Press, Toronto, 1973

Lancaster, Bruce. Bright to the Wanderer; Little, Brown
and Company; Boston, 1942

Leechman, Douglas. Native Tribes of Canada; W.J. Gage,
Toronto, no date

Lizars, Kathleen Macfarlane. The Valley of The Humber;
1615-1913; Coles Publishing Company, Toronto, 1974
(Coles Canadian Collection)

Masters, D.C. The Rise of Toronto; University of Toronto
Press, Toronto, 1974

Meredith, Alden. Mary Rosedale and Gossip of Little
York. Graphic Publishers Limited, Ottawa, 1928

McWhirter, Norris and Ross. The Guiness Book of
World Records, Bantam Books, March, 1976

Middleton, Jesse Edgar. Municipality of Toronto, A
History, Vol. 1; Dominion Publishing Company, Toronto
and New York, 1923 (Toronto Central Library)

Middleton, J.E. and F. Landon. Province of Ontario:
A History, Vol. 1 & 2, 1615-1927; Dominion Publishing
Company, 1927 (City Hall Archives)

Mitchell, John. The Settlement of York County; Municipal Corporation of the County of York, printed by
Charters Publishing Company, no date.

Moodie, Susanna. Life in the Clearings, edited by Robert McDougall; MacMillan (Canada), Toronto, 1959

Mulvany, Charles Pelham. Toronto: Past and Present; a Handbook of the City; Ontario Reprint Press, Toronto, 1970. (Originally published in 1884 by W.E. Caiger)

O'Brien, Mary. The Journals of Mary O'Brien, 1828-1838, edited by Audrey Saunders Miller; Macmillan (Canada), Toronto, 1968

Ontario. Department of Public Records and Archives; Historic Ontario; Department of Tourism and Information, Toronto, no date

Pearson, W.H. Recollections and Records of Toronto of Old. William Briggs Company, 1914.

Reamen, George Elmore. The Trail of the Black Walnut; McClelland and Stewart, Toronto, 1957

Robertson, John Ross. Old Toronto; a Selection of Exerpts From Landmarks of Toronto; Macmillan, Toronto, 1954

Robertson's Landmarks, Vol. 5 & 6. Toronto 1834-1914 & Old Town of York 1792-1883; Mika Publishing Company, Belleville, Ontario. (Originally published by J. Ross Robertson, 1898) (City Hall Archives)

Robinson, Percy James. Toronto During the French Regime; University of Toronto Press, Toronto 1965

Saywell, John Tupper. Canada Past And Present; Clarke Irwin, Toronto 1969

Scadding, Henry. Toronto of Old; (original version) Adam, Stevenson & Company, Toronto 1873

Scadding, Henry. Toronto of Old (abridged and edited by F.H. Armstrong); Oxford University Press, Toronto 1966

Scadding, Henry and Charles Dent. Toronto Past and Present:Hunter Rose and Company, Toronto, 1884 (City Hall Archives)

Scott, Duncan Campbell. John Graves Simcoe; Makers of Canada, Anniversary Edition, Vol. 4, Oxford University Press, Toronto, 1926

Simcoe, Elizabeth. The Diary of Mrs. John Graves Simcoe; Coles Publishing Company, Toronto, 1973. (Coles Canadiana Collection) Originally published by W. Briggs, Toronto, 1911

Smith, H. Footprints in Time; House of Grant (Canada), 1964

Smith, William Henry. Smith's Canadian Gazetteer; H & W. Rowesell, Toronto, 1846

Smith, William Loe. The Pioneers of Old Ontario; Morang and Company Limited, Toronto, 1923. (Makers of Canada; Parkman Edition, new series)

Spelt, Jacob. Toronto; Collier-Macmillan, Toronto, 1973

Statistical Account of Upper Canada, Vol. 1. Robert F. Gourlay; Johnson Reprint Corporation, 1966. (Originally published by Limpkin and Marshall Stationers Court, London, England, 1822) (Toronto Central Library, Baldwin Room)

Strachan, James. A Visit To the Province of Upper Canada in 1819; Johnson Reprint Corporation, New York, 1968 (Originally printed by D. Chalmers and Company, 1820)

Tiffany, Orrin Edward. The Canadian Rebellion of 1837-38; Coles Publishing Company, Toronto, 1972 (Coles Canadiana Collection)

Toronto Transportation Commission. Transit in Toronto; TTC, 1967

Newspapers

Barrie Magnet, The, August 6, 1847

Colonial Advocate, The, September 24, 1829

Enterprise, The, January 25, 1967

Fort Frances Times, The, June 23, 30, 1965, April 27, 1966

New Market Era, The, April 7, 1899

Niagara Canada Constellation, The, August 23, 1799. December 14, 1799, December 20, 1800

North American, The, August 20, 1850

Smith's Gazetteer, 1799

Toronto British Colonist, The, August 2, 1843

Toronto Daily Patriot, The, October 10, 1850

Toronto Examiner, The, August 2, 1843, August 21, 28, 1850

Toronto Globe, The, April 14, July 10, 1847

Toronto Globe and Mail, The, March 6, October 7, 9, 15, 19, 20, 1954, February 26, 1955, February 28, 1961, August 12, 1964, May 30, 1974, April 5, 17, May 31, August 27, September 3, 6, 8, 20, 22, 1975

Toronto Mail and Empire, The, June 3, 1931

Toronto Star, The, October 15, 1954, July 28, 1962, July 5, 1969, July 22, August 13, 1971, January 5, February 12, August 26, 1972, February 21, May 11, May 15, June 2, June 20, 28, August 20, 1973,May 27, June 20, November 16, 1974, April 5, 28, May 17, 31, June 2, 3, 4, 5, 6, 7, 10, 11, 12, 13, 14, 16, 17, 18, 20, 21, 23, 25, 28, 30, July 1, 2, 4, 5, 12, 19, August 2, 11, 14, 20, 21, 26, 27, 29, 30, September 1, 2, 4, 5, 6, 8, 12, 20, 23, 25, 27, 29, 30, October 2, 3, 7, 11, 19, 21, 27, 28, 29, November 11, December 5, 8, 9, 11, 1975, January 1, 3, February 3, 7, March 6, April 5, 6, 7, 24, May 11, 21, 1976

Toronto Sun, The, May 4, June 4, 8, 11, 30, August 17, September 7, 28, October 5, 19, 26, November 2, 1975, January 11, 25, 1976

Toronto Telegram, The, May 16, July 4, 1931, March 16, 1935, February 28, 1969, January 28, 1970, May 31, 1971

United Church Observer, The, July, 1975

Upper Canada Gazette, The, March 9, August 10, 1799, March 1, December 20, 1800, June 12, 1802, June 13, 1808, August, 1825

Weekly Register, The, August, 1825

York Courier of Upper Canada, The, June 16, 1832

York Oracle, The, March 21, 1801

Index

155